NOT BEING GOD

NOT BEING GOD

A Collaborative Autobiography

GIANNI VATTIMO *with* **PIERGIORGIO PATERLINI**

Translated by **WILLIAM MCCUAIG**

COLUMBIA UNIVERSITY PRESS NEW YORK

COLUMBIA UNIVERSITY PRESS
Publishers Since 1893
New York   Chichester, West Sussex

COPYRIGHT © 2009 COLUMBIA UNIVERSITY PRESS
ORIGINALLY COPYRIGHT © 2008 ALIBERTI EDITORE S.R.L.

Library of Congress Cataloging-in-Publication Data
Vattimo, Gianni, 1936–
[non essere Dio. English]
Not being God : a collaborative autobiography / Gianni Vattimo with
Piergiorgio Paterlini ; translated by William McCuaig.
p. cm.
ISBN 978-0-231-14720-0 (cloth : alk. paper)—ISBN 978-0-231-51957-1
(e-book)
1. Vattimo, Gianni, 1936– 2. Philosophers—Italy—Biography. I. Paterlini,
Piergiorgio, 1954– II. Title.
B3654.V384A3 2009
195—dc22
[B]

2008045981

Columbia University Press books are printed on permanent
and durable acid-free paper.

This book is printed on paper with recycled content.
Printed in the United States of America

c 10 9 8 7 6 5 4 3 2 1

DESIGN BY: **MARTIN N. HINZE**

Dear Professor, in the end I would much rather be a Basel professor than God; but I have not dared push my private egoism so far as to desist for its sake from the creation of the world.

FRIEDRICH NIETZSCHE, LETTER TO JACOB BURCKHARDT
FROM TURIN, JANUARY 6, 1889

CONTENTS

ANALOGIES

Gianni Vattimo is the philosopher who has fought all his life against the confines of object-ivity and the absolutes that imprison us. This book—which tries to recount, in a comprehensible manner, the life and thought of Gianni Vattimo, who turned seventy in 2006, when it was written—cannot, therefore, advance claims to object-ivity, to absolute truth. Besides, it is a strange book. We both know it, Vattimo and I. We made the choice. It is not an autobiography in the usual sense, because I wrote it, and it's not a biography because Vattimo is cosigning it and speaks in the first person.

So how did we arrive at this fused impasto of two voices, two persons? Ultimately, because I wanted to do it (long live subjectivity) and because Gianni Vattimo agreed to do it with me. But above all, because this necessary (auto)biography is something he—who writes so engagingly, unlike many of his colleagues—would never have written. The idea would never have occurred to him, and he would not have written it anyway. So this note already forms part of the (auto)biography. It states fact number one about Gianni Vattimo: Gianni Vattimo is someone who would never have written his own autobiography for himself.

Over his long philosophical trajectory, which began and is constantly interpenetrated with the theme of Being, Gianni Vattimo has come to the view that Being eventuates for us in language, or rather in human conversation, in "colloquy."

This (auto)biography comes about exactly so: in human colloquy between the great philosopher and me.

Lately Vattimo has been defending, and accepts as positive and fertile, a certain indeterminacy in history and in the writing of books. Resonances, even, and perhaps something more. Because anyone telling his own story selects, consciously and unconsciously; to use a favorite expression of Gianni Vattimo, he "goes and finds out" (*va a sapere*). And this selection is obviously overlaid with my own. With a certain claim to honesty and objectivity, if not object-ivity, in an attitude of listening, something especially dear as well to Vattimo the man and Vattimo the thinker.

The one thing that can't be said about this book is that its structure does not respect, indeed virtually replicate—in a way quite unexpected and surprising, even for me—the existential, human, and philosophical trajectory of the person doing the telling.

Piergiorgio Paterlini

NOT BEING GOD

1 | INCIPIT

My dear Stefano,

Does growing older ease the pain of living? Does it make us less capable of suffering, and so of loving and experiencing passion? Does it make us more cynical, harder, less sensitive? I ask myself this today, at the onset of my old age.

I fear that the answer is yes, and I reproach myself for it.

On my seventieth birthday I spent the day—you weren't there, as usual, I note with a touch of bitterness, but with much greater tenderness for you, as you know, and acceptance of your being so young and beautiful—I was saying, on my seventieth birthday I spent the day with a few friends in the little house I have at Roquebrune, drinking terrible wine and sending e-mails saying, "Today I bid a sad farewell to sixty-nine."

Then I took a fall. Like a moron. Like a baby. Stumbled, slipped, I don't know. What I do know is that I banged my head hard and got a huge bump. I keep asking myself: Is this the first sign of dementia? Have I got a brain tumor? Is this kind of thing normal at my age?

I know well enough that people will adapt to anything sooner or later to keep on living. But though this is immensely reassuring, it does make it seem as though things, even the most important things, thereby lose value. It's, how shall I put it, a little . . . disappointing.

When Sergio, who had lived with Gianpiero and me for close to fifteen years, and then alone with me for another eleven, died, the pain I felt was less acute than when Gianpiero died. And for that I do blame myself. I really have the impression that I felt less pain, that I suffered less, with less intensity.

Then again, if somebody had told me beforehand what I was going to go through during the devastating illness and prolonged agony of Gianpiero, all the thousand little everyday things, I wouldn't have been able to stand the thought. Yet here I am. So it's really true, then, you can get through anything, adapt to anything? It's this that makes me suspect that maybe everything loses a bit of value, a bit of intensity with the passing of time. If you don't actually die from love, perhaps it wasn't such a great love after all, or maybe it was. So there it is, a question to which I haven't yet found the answer.

Today, if someone brings me sad news, even very sad news, like the sudden discovery that they have a tumor, as someone did recently, my first reaction is: I've already been through worse. Then of course I do still suffer for the things one has to suffer for, and yet. . . .

When it comes to public affairs, I'm not so tentative. The fact that I am so angry at the state of the world doesn't, I think, arise solely from my entirely private regret for my own lost youth. My students, who unlike me are not seventy years old, often have the same outlook on things as I do, so it must not depend on age. In any case, I try to pay close attention; I go over the list again and again from the beginning, trying to figure out if it's all in my head, or if there's more to it. And these appear to me objective facts, not things imagined by a peevish old man: the left today is just pathetic, from D'Alema to Rutelli to Bertinotti; and, scandalously, the CIA can now run around Italy doing whatever it likes as never before. And the war, and Bush, and Berlusconi. . . . I don't really think you can dismiss all that as the aches and pains of old age. Not mine anyway.

Lebenszeit und Weltzeit is the title of Hans Blumenberg's book on Edmund Husserl. The tempo of life and the tempo of the world. It's clear that we are always living at these two tempos simultaneously. Nevertheless it is still possible to state something about the present. Not something absolute, but something that is true, true for me, true for us, shareable and verifiable, albeit within the paradigms of our historicity, our culture, our language.

Weak thought is not unconnected with these queries. From "weak thought" to "weak passion"? Perhaps. But not in the sense of unimportant, just as weak thought is quite the opposite of "unimportant," whatever others may say. A motto I've repeated for years, smash down the walls instead of smashing your head (like I almost did on my birthday, and not metaphorically), might also signify this kind of self-protection against pain. Yet the suspicion nags. A slight disquiet.

I think and say all these things without taking myself too seriously. I live with a moderate, almost apocalyptic, optimism. Who knows if things will go better? I have always been a believer in providence (whether the providence of God or of things in general I don't know) but I'm certainly not all that pessimistic about the chances of the world going to ruin.

I don't think that everything will necessarily keep getting worse and worse. I don't have complete faith in myself, or history, or my contemporaries. Luckily the world hasn't been entrusted either to me or exclusively to Bush.

I sometimes listen to that poem by Bertolt Brecht that Kurt Weill set to music: "On the floor of the Moldau the stones roll along / Three Kaisers lie buried in Prague. / In this world nothing remains the same / The longest of nights comes to an end."

And for sure, I feel free like never before. Free to say whatever I think. That I do. And this is one of the many things for which I'm not forgiven, either by my enemies or by my friends. I can say that D'Alema belongs on the scrap heap, and I can tell *Vanity Fair* that I have fallen in love with a cubist in his twenties. I do it because of this exceptional freedom (which might also be a dividend of old age), not because of a taste for provocation or exhibitionism, or even out of the kind of capriciousness that old people need to be protected against, like children. People reproach me: "Why on earth do you do it?" Or: "What's driving you? You could be an august sage and you flaunt yourself like that." I just grin. I do it because I feel free. Because I am free. And it's something I cherish. Finally. No more fear, no more mediation, no more vulnerability to pressure, no more fear of hurting my mother or Gianpiero. With no church or party. How sweet it is.

2 | LAST THINGS

No, I have no fear of death. My own death has almost no importance to me.

The really scandalous death you have to bear isn't your own, it's that of others close to you.

Gianpiero's death scandalizes me. Sergio's death scandalizes me. So does my mother's, my aunt's, my sister's. The uncompletedness of their lives.

Sergio wrote a few important things in art history, and Gianpiero some beautiful books in comparative literature: these are the things I regret they were unable to bring to fruition.

I am simply unable to imagine that death is the end of everything.

It's my aunt who makes me so sure of this, more than the thought of, say, Dante Alighieri. Who cares about the immortality or the eternity of Dante? He has already had his form of immortality.

But is it conceivable that my aunt—a lady, a single lady in fact, who died at age seventy-five after having passed her whole life alone, perhaps because a youthful love affair ended badly, who remained a spinster and worked in a factory all her life—can be dead without leaving a trace? That I can't believe. Aunt Angiolina stayed in Turin alone during the war, working in a place where they made socks, Signor Galoppo's sock factory (she went "at a gallop" we used to say, because we liked the play on words), while my mother and sister and I took refuge in Calabria, where my father came from. She got up every morning and took the number 8 bus, because she lived near the Martinetto, close enough to hear the bursts of machine-gun fire when they executed partisans at dawn. She would leave the house with her lunch pail, go to the factory, work, and come home from the factory. She was another person who never got too upset, I think, otherwise she would have died a lot sooner, of fright. But to think that that person should be dead without there being any more trace of her for eternity seems to me a scandal not only intolerable but also unthinkable. Who cares if Dante Alighieri is dead and buried? We have his works. But my aunt? Let's not be ridiculous. Not my aunt.

My master, Luigi Pareyson, used to say, "If I were sure there were nothing after death, how happy I'd be." A statement like that is inconceivable for me. It could only have come from a man who bore within himself an immense fear of sin and a terrifying sense of evil. Two things that luckily I've never had.

Hans Georg Gadamer used to say about death, "Man is a being who sometimes drowses and sometimes sleeps."

Once I spoke about it with Richard Rorty, too, when we were traveling together in Utah. We both agreed: dying is rotten only because it leaves you wondering what will happen afterward.

And Gianpiero always used to remind me of a saying of Károly Kerényi, the great Hungarian scholar of mythology, whom he knew and to whom he introduced me during a trip to Switzerland, where Kerényi lived: "Before I was born I didn't know that the world was so interesting. Who knows what I'll find after death?"

3 | CLOSENESS

Every Sunday I go to the cemetery—the Cimitero Monumentale, near here—where the tombstones of Gianpiero and Sergio are, one above the other, and an empty slot waiting for me. I feel at peace. I continue to feel a great closeness to them, something that doesn't happen to me with anyone else, not even with my mother or sister.

When I saw my sister dead, in that absurd bed at the Maria Vittoria Hospital, I really thought: look, she's in another world now, in another time; she's closer to Julius Caesar than to me.

With Gianpiero and Sergio I've never noticed such a dimension of *otherness*. And I tell myself: now nothing more can happen to them, nothing bad, nothing ugly.

And what's the worst that can happen to me, ultimately? I hope for a death without dreadful suffering. I might get arrested, but in that case, put me in a cell with a beautiful young prisoner. Don't put me in with Vittorio Emanuele—please, not that.

This absence of anxiety also brings me to see that it isn't true that everything is worse today than before.

Today, not being overly fearful, I know that someone worse could arrive, or return. Someone even worse than D'Alema or Berlusconi or Bush.

I was born in Turin in January 1936. I saw the war. I lived through the war. And I remember it well. In 1939 I was three; in 1945 I was nine. If I were told that tomorrow the bombing and the sirens and the blackouts were coming back, well, that, I know, would be "worse."

CLOSENESS

4 | THE UNTIED SHOELACE

I've lived through some tough times. I've heard bombs falling overhead. Air-raid sirens. When I was five I was already going to school, and I recall one day when we had to race for the bomb shelter. I had one shoelace undone, and I was in real trouble because we had to run and I couldn't tie my shoes by myself. A little girl helped me.

Another night it was a miracle I didn't get blown away along with my whole family. By chance we were in the shelter beside our own. Next morning we came out and our house had been razed to the ground. Completely destroyed. Like the whole neighborhood, for that matter.

I remember people digging away in search of the rarest and therefore most precious thing: mattresses. My aunt was digging, and my mother was helping her while keeping an eye on me and my sister, who was eight years older than me.

With the house gone, we were evacuated, first to my uncle's at Bricherasio, in the countryside near here. Then to the south of Italy. Our relatives there wrote us that life was better, that there were chickens, a garden, in other words, enough to eat. We went to Cetraro, near the town of Paola; our quarter was called Citino. We left on a night train, traveled for two days. It was night again when we arrived, in utter terror because they were bombing the rail lines.

My memories of Calabria are still very intense and very beautiful. We took the sheep and goats out to pasture.

My little cousin Rita and I made a pretend garden, a first try.

For a while we were all camped out together in one big room, and we ate on the threshing floor. Then we changed houses a couple of times, and finally we found a place to rent in Cetraro, part of a large villa, with a common kitchen on the top floor. It was owned by the Rossi sisters, Donna Rosina and Donna Teresina, who spent their time squabbling and claimed they had a brother at Rome who was Mussolini's doctor.

I remember a political exile from Lombardy who used to visit us and played strange games. And the first person my sister fell in love with. He left for Argentina, and we lost track of him forever.

I went to church, and I was an altar boy, like everyone else. I was in love with a little girl named Filomena, whom everybody called Menella, and I tried to find a way to tell her.

I went to school, too. Some distance away. I used to set out on foot with my friend Delio down through the woods to the school. I was supposed to be in second grade, but I was far enough ahead that they put me in third. But I didn't know enough for third, I couldn't do division, and I used to get my fingers whacked hard. Eventually, though, I was top of the class. I wanted to be a writer, and I was already playing the intellectual.

I read books published in the Scala d'Oro collection, such as *Il romanzo di Fanfulla* (The Tale of Fanfulla).

We had a stupendous terrace from which you could see Stromboli. I used to write up there, I don't remember what; I remember I set up an office of sorts.

We even used to stage plays, all my little friends and I. We got together in the cellar of the son of a sergeant in the Carabinieri, a rich family of local notables. The son, Tonino, was one of my best friends. He and I wrote a comedy, *Senza cuore* (Without a Heart).

At dusk I used to hang around with Alduccio, the doctor's son, in front of the pharmacy where the local men gathered, sitting on wooden stools. I used to discuss the war and politics too.

But I also played football. I was playing with a ball made of cloth when the news came about the German surrender. We were anxious for the war to end so we could finally play with a real football, made of leather.

Then the shouting in the streets: peace, peace. A large procession formed, some people were even dragging themselves along on their knees. It was May.

In September they assembled all of us evacuees at Paola, in a species of internment camp inside a school. A week of waiting while they put together the special train to take us back up north.

We returned to Turin.

I spoke nothing but Calabrese dialect, and that made me a *terrone* (southerner) and earned me a few beatings from my schoolmates.

5 | RORSCHACH TEST

At the Liceo Classico Gioberti, a high school for the humanities, our professor liked history, not philosophy. For a textbook, he had chosen the one with the fewest pages.

I, however, had my own personal master. Apart from school. A Thomist, an ultra-Thomist: Monsignor Pietro Caramello. A man who thought it was too progressive even to call himself a neo-Thomist. He used to protest that he was a Thomist period, forget the "neo." He edited the works of Saint Thomas for the publisher Marietti, and he was the chaplain of the Sindone (the Shroud of Turin), practically a retainer of the House of Savoy. But I don't believe the Shroud was very important to him. He certainly respected it as a relic, but he would never have undergone martyrdom for the Shroud. He was a philosopher.

A philosopher. A master. But also a spiritual director, a friend. Maybe the person who did the most to bring me up, who was immensely fond of me and of whom I was immensely fond.

It was my parish priests who first sent me to him, who knows why. Maybe they thought they had stumbled upon the philosopher's stone.

After I graduated from university we drifted apart, and it is one of my regrets that he died while I was in America. I was moved recently when I recognized him in a television documentary, where he is seen opening the reliquary and spreading out the sacred fabric.

Don Pietro was a really notable personality, one of the men who knew neoscholastic philosophy best, or scholastic tout court, as he would have it.

From high school until the end of university, I went to confession with him twice a week. And we took trips to the mountains alone together more than once, to the Certosa di Pesio for example, weeks divided between spiritual exercises and study. I would study, and he would help me when I asked him. Intense years, years of ardent philosophical debate. I would always bring up the problem of the just war. But above all, even then, I could not accept the idea of an immutable "natural order" (in which, apart from anything else, there would have been no place for me). And I wrestled with the idea of "natural theology," which drove the Catholic Church straight into the arms of the right, whereas I was on the left. Catholic, but on the left.

I don't believe I ever told him about my homosexuality. He had me make vows, though. He would say, "You will now make a vow of chastity for a week." Or he would have me recite the rosary with my hands under my knees. In sum, lots of affection and a little dose of self-mortification.

And I really can't explain why one day he sent me to a psychiatrist, still an eminent faculty member in the University of Turin, who received me with great solemnity in his study, along with a colleague.

They gave me the Rorschach test and sent me away, promising to get back to me. Never heard from them again. Maybe I was a hopeless case.

My great master in university was Luigi Pareyson. Maestro and lifelong friend.

In my university years, I didn't yet know what to think. I dallied with the Thomism of Caramello and with Pareyson's philosophy, and like many left-wing Catholics at that time I read Emmanuel Mounier and Jacques Maritain, looking for a way out of the jaws of the trap formed by liberal capitalism and the bureaucratized communism of the Soviet Union. In short, I didn't want to be identified either as a liberal or a Marxist. And—like Maritain—I was especially interested in criticizing the dogmas of modernity.

At age twenty-three, in 1959, I took my bachelor's degree with a thesis on the "concept of doing in Aristotle." Two years later it was published, revised and corrected.

I went for a talk with my master Pareyson, and I told him, "I'd like to study Adorno." I had read the *Minima Moralia,* and to be honest, had understood about ten percent of it. Pareyson replied, "Forget Adorno, read something more up to date, study Nietzsche."

Okay, I'll study Friedrich Nietzsche.

The summer after my degree I went to the mountains alone— another great passion of mine, running through my whole existence—to a shelter three thousand meters up, above Cervinia, at

Colle del Theodulo, near Plateau Rosa, bringing with me the French translation of Nietzsche's *Unfashionable Observations,* especially the essay entitled "On the Utility and Liability of History for Life," meaning historical studies, historiography.

I would ski in the morning, then eat lunch and chat with a cornetist from the Vienna Opera who was also staying at the shelter, and then study Nietzsche.

An epic summer! I discovered Nietzsche's critique of historicism, his reflections against modernity, and this image of his that remained fundamental for me: modern man is wandering around in history as if it were a theme park or a storehouse of theatrical masks, trying on this one and that one.

The previous December I had read the *Letter on Humanism* that Martin Heidegger wrote "against" Sartre. An illumination, a real conversion experience. The most important turn—or rather twofold turn, together with the discovery of Nietzsche—of my speculative experience. There's no doubt that for me it all begins there.

Heidegger writes: we are not on a plane where there is mankind alone, but on which there is above all and principally Being.

This business about Being intrigued me, because it seemed to be receptive to my religious heritage, and more than that, I saw in it a philosophical (and existential and political) prospect of liberty, of liberation. Not with stark clarity at first, but that was certainly what drew me.

So what happens? Just while I am studying Nietzsche, out come two big volumes on Nietzsche by Heidegger. Naturally I can't go further into Nietzsche without knowing what Heidegger has to say.

So I plunge into Heidegger. And that was it, the second great erotico-philosophical adventure of my life.

I read him in German, Heidegger, taking systematic notes on small green sheets of paper from the Banco San Paolo. You know, recycled paper. I've always been a fanatic about reusing paper.

Those little green pages with my notes, I still have them today.

7 | BEING

Not only have we forgotten what Being means, we have forgotten that we have forgotten. Heidegger places this sentence from Plato's *Sophist* at the beginning of his *Being and Time,* the book with which he forced himself onto the attention of the philosophical world and the general culture at the end of the 1920s.

Heidegger reads Nietzsche, and as he does, he reconstructs the history of Plato's Ideas down to modernity, to today, meaning down to positivistic scientific experimentation, which for Heidegger is the height of the forgetting of Being.

I began to worry at this problem, and it's the thread running through all my philosophical work.

Heidegger, I found, was contradictory about this. Or, at any rate, he didn't succeed in drawing out all the consequences of his own intuitions. Right there was the starting point of all my own research, my personal reading, my interpretation, of Heidegger, and naturally of Nietzsche. It still is.

Heidegger doesn't really know how to solve this problem of the forgetting of Being. He oscillates between nostalgia and awareness that the whole history of philosophy in the West, metaphysics, is over and that it's a good thing it is. Time to move on. Because on one hand, Being is the most important thing there is; it's precisely what allows man to be, it's what illuminates reality. Yet at the same time Plato's Being, the Ideas existing in Hyperuranium, which then become the Cartesian *cogito,* the absolute truth, the Christian paradise, and so on down to scientific positivism, all these putatively objective truths are the negation of Being and so deserve merely to die.

Nietzsche rejoices in this dissolution of the "real world," because for him it means liberation: finally we are living in a world in which there are no more objective limits, and precisely in order to bear this liberty we have to become overmen.

Nietzsche registers the death of God without any nostalgia. As though he were heaving a sigh of relief, he writes "God is dead, now we wish that many Gods may live."

In sum, whereas Nietzsche is quite content to be a nihilist, Heidegger is a little less so. In fact, he wishes he weren't. Actually he is, and will be all his life.

There is a general misunderstanding to the effect that Nietzsche's strong affirmation that "God is dead" is a profession of atheism. That's not it. Nietzsche does not affirm that God does not exist. He could never affirm that, because it would amount to another absolute truth entirely equivalent to the affirmation that "God exists." It's the point of view that is different. Wherever there is an absolute there is still always metaphysics, meaning a supreme principle, exactly what Nietzsche has discovered has become superfluous. "God is dead" signifies that there is no ultimate foundation.

Though Heidegger doesn't want to acknowledge this, Nietzsche's affirmation has the same meaning as his own polemic against metaphysics, in other words against the whole European philosophical tradition from Parmenides on, that believes it can grasp an ultimate foundation of reality in the form of an objective structure located outside of time and history. Heidegger's great revolution is the refusal, in the name of liberty, of a stable, objective, structural conception of Being. If we are bearers of hopes, feelings, fear, projects . . . finite beings, with a past and a future, and not just appearances, then Being cannot be thought in terms of objectivistic metaphysics.

For me this is the first step, a beginning, nameless but crucial, of what twenty years later would be called "weak thought."

You breathe good air up there at three thousand meters. The oxygen sometimes makes you feel drunk. I was through forever with any form of Thomism, drunk on freedom.

8 | EPOCHS

There is something else that stirs my emotions and makes me feel a connection to Martin Heidegger.

At a certain point I began to read Michel Foucault (but you know, when you read Foucault, more than anything else you invent what you think he meant to say, because you grasp little or nothing)—anyway, I was reading Foucault and thinking about Theodor Adorno's "epochs," the fact that he often speaks of "constellations."

Heidegger, too, imagines history as flashes. Sudden illuminations. Occurrences. (The noun in Italian is *accadimenti,* literally things that befall, that come about, that take place. And the Italian verb that captures the meaning with the greatest idiomatic force is *darsi,* the reflexive form of *dare,* to give, which signifies "to occur, to come about, to eventuate.") Within these flashes time is articulated into historical epochs. But in Heidegger the epoch is a suspension of time, an instantaneous fracture.

Time is not continuous. As in Saint Augustine, in a way, time is linked to existence, and to the existence of mankind. And Being illuminates itself in different ways in different epochs, epochs that are discontinuous. Being is nothing other than certain historical horizons lighting up from time to time, with no visible continuity between one epoch and another.

The cornetist with the Vienna Opera watched my face lighting up, and not just because of the bright sunshine. He kept telling me the story of his life and smiling at me with his eyes.

9 | THE IMPOSSIBLE RETURN

So Heidegger "regrets" that we have forgotten Being. But he doesn't see clearly how to get out of this. What to do?

Years later I succeeded in giving a relatively full answer of my own, going beyond Heidegger while remaining faithful to him in substance. Above all, I came to understand the moments at which the great German philosopher gives in to nostalgia and imagines a possible return of Being that wouldn't openly contradict everything he has thought and written, and the points at which, on the contrary, he supplies a possible confirmation of my "nihilistic" reading.

Right from that first impact, though, I understood—and asked myself—a few things.

If you forget a telephone number, you have to try to remember it, end of story. But with Being? Heidegger speaks of metaphysics as the forgetting of Being because, instead of posing the problem of what Being means, it has reduced Being to an object, even when it calls it "God," which may be the most perfect Being, but is still always an "object" among others.

So what are we to do? What does Heidegger want to do? Does he want us to remember Being? But can Being be remembered? I am not the only one intrigued and fascinated by this question. It torments all Heidegger's interpreters, especially the ones who are reading Nietzsche at the same time.

It is a genuine problem. Because if Being is simply something that was, and that we have forgotten but might remember, at that precise moment it is no longer Being, it is like a potato, or any object whatsoever set there before us. So it is hard for Heidegger to imagine the way out of the forgetting of Being as the recovery of memory following amnesia, even centuries-long amnesia. To remember it means to appropriate it to oneself, and at that point we are back to objectivation.

Clearly Heidegger hates the idea of Being as something present, there in front of us, because that would make it an object. Therefore, he cannot think that it returns in that sense; all he can think is that Being itself alters its stance toward us, that it does eventuate for us again, not "in presence" but rather as rents in history that inaugurate new epochs. Great works of art—he privileges these, and I was swayed by that at first, though later I came to different conclusions—are primarily what inaugurate new epochs for Heidegger. But without continuity with the rest of history, with the illuminations that went before.

Therefore there never was a "before," a before metaphysics, a before Plato, when Being was right in front of us, and which we ought simply to go looking for.

For Heidegger there can be only one answer: it is not we who are bound to remember; rather, it will depend on Being itself, in what might be called a logic of redemption, but also of social revolution, to change our situation of historical forgetting of Being.

My own answer, many years later, was: we cannot remember Being; all we can do is remember having forgotten it.

In any case, in order to respect the fundamental proposition of Heidegger—that is, the difference between Being and something objectively given, whether it be the Ideas of Plato, Paradise in the Christian ages, or the scientific experiment in the epoch of science—we simply have to suppose, even if Heidegger never arrived at this, that the only possible history of Being is the growing lighter, the losing weight (*alleggerimento*) of Being itself. The history of Being is the history of how objective truth gradually dissolves; therefore, it is nihilism, the history of nihilism as sketched by Nietzsche. Being is confirmed as that which illuminates things without being identified with things. A lamp that illuminates a chair, that allows the chair to "be there," but that is not the chair. Growing lighter, therefore. But also: growing more distant.

How do we emerge from the forgetting of Being? Not through preparing for its return, only through thinking its history as that of something that is withdrawing, growing ever more distant. If there is a history of Being, it is a history of distancing, not of drawing closer. Being illuminates to the extent that it withdraws.

Dietrich Bonhoeffer comes to mind: "A God who is, is not." Hard to get a grip on. But really beautiful.

10 | DEBUT

On November 28, 1961, I was invited to give an important lecture at the Biblioteca Filosofica of Turin, an association directed by Augusto Guzzo, who had as it happens been the master of Luigi Pareyson.

Back then, such occasions were real events, events for the whole city, not just academic affairs. All the most important philosophers, the *monstres sacres,* were in the front row: Nicola Abbagnano, Pietro Chiodi, Carlo Mazzantini, Augusto Guzzo, Pietro Rossi, Carlo Augusto Viano. Luigi Pareyson, naturally. And Norberto Bobbio. And Michele Pellegrino, who taught ancient Christian literature, and was later to become one of the most prestigious and innovative archbishops of Turin.

And there was Turin's high society.

The title was "Who Is Heidegger's Nietzsche?" In short, I was presenting Heidegger to the public, and at the same time to Pietro Chiodi—the Italian translator of *Being and Time,* who had known Heidegger for a lot longer than I had.

What I had to say in that lecture became chapter 1 of a book of mine that came out in 1963, my first important book and my first book period if we leave out the one on Aristotle: *Essere, storia, e linguaggio in Heidegger* (Being, History, and Language in Heidegger). That book and the one on Nietzsche that I wrote ten years later are still the two fundamental moments for my formation and for the construction of my personal philosophical theory.

I was twenty-five, and my narcissism was at its peak. I was moved, but above all very excited and happy. For the first time I was declaring myself as someone who was really doing philosophy, a philosopher with his own theoretical stance. Not just a solid researcher, not just a historian of philosophy.

I haven't yet told you why and in what sense and in what way I was a Catholic, from age twelve to age twenty-four or twenty-five. But I know that I stopped being one when I no longer read the Italian newspapers. My religious commitment was so much interwoven with my philosophical and political commitment that, when I lost contact with Italian politics, boom, it was all over, painlessly, just like it began. Even if a lot of passion was consumed in the interval.

After graduating, I won the prestigious Humboldt Fellowship for two consecutive years. So I went to live in Germany for months at a time, in Heidelberg. Eight hundred marks amounted to a rich postdoctoral fellowship at that period.

I lived in a room on the top floor of a small house near the city's old bridge, with a terrace overlooking the Neckar River.

I traveled back to Turin once a month, but that's all. And *La Stampa* was two days old by the time it reached Heidelberg. . . . After having spent years and years getting up at dawn to go to mass—before school, before the office, before university lectures—I continued going on Sunday for a while in the church of the Holy Spirit, near the university, and then I just stopped.

Heidelberg was another great intellectual adventure. It was there that I really began to work out my philosophy.

At Heidelberg I attended the lectures of the great philosopher Hans Georg Gadamer, Heidegger's student, whom I later translated and made better known in Italy. Habermas's pronunciation I couldn't understand, but Gadamer I could follow; he spoke a particularly clear brand of German, at any rate in the lectures he gave for his "formal" course. I had more trouble following him when he was speaking to the handful of members of his "reserved seminar," and afterward when we used to go with him in winter to an old tavern to eat goulash and black bread and drink wine, and to his house in the hills in summer.

So I was frequenting Gadamer, the other lectures very little, and the library a lot, where I could read texts I wouldn't have found in Italy. I worked on my Heidegger book. Most evenings I stayed in, supping on bread, butter, and salami and trying to smoke a pipe, because I remembered the ease with which Umberto Eco used to handle his pipe when we lived together in Milan.

Although a decent knowledge of languages has helped me along in life, I confess that vis-à-vis Gadamer I felt like a worm. As far as I could tell, the only one who understood less than me was a beautiful prince from some African tribe, whom I tried to seduce. Unsuccessfully, because of the language barrier. The other students all seemed to me exceedingly clever, and perhaps they were—today they all hold chairs in Germany with major academic careers behind them.

Gadamer was my other great maestro, along with Pareyson. And a friend, though an ironic one who always managed to keep his distance.

I have to admit that the second year I went to Heidelberg mostly to pick up my stipend. Then I would return to Italy and use the money to live on as Pareyson's assistant. But when Gadamer began his course I showed up respectfully to greet him, and he said, "Oh, are you still here?" with that slightly mocking air of his.

Years later I was asked to give a course at the University of Louvain, the same course Gadamer had given, and the first thing I did was ring him up. And he—the great narcissist—pointed out to me that it wasn't the same university, because in the meantime they had split it between Leuven in Flanders (the A-list university where he had taught) and Louvain-la-Neuve in Wallonia (the B-list university where I was going to teach).

Later, though, I was his first translator into a language other than German (something Paul Ricoeur acknowledges, mentioning me in his French translation), and I spent many a summer afternoon at his house discussing my queries about the translation.

I finished *Verità e metodo,* my translation of *Wahrheit und Methode,* in 1969, five hundred pages of wonderful training for me. I returned to Heidelberg, and this time Gianpiero, whom I had met the year before, came with me. I spent many hours with Gadamer and "assimilated" him as a person too.

Whenever he came to Italy he always rang me up.

I was one of the three philosophers asked to deliver a speech in his honor on his hundredth birthday. It was 2000, and Gadamer had two more years to live. At the end of the ceremony, I remember, he drank a whole bottle of Calvados. To him—with his combination of distance and affection, snobbishness and great generosity and intellectual honesty, all of which I find in his letters, which are full of punctual and respectful observations—I owe one of the strongest emotions of my life as a philosopher. It was Gadamer, the great Gadamer, who, when he was listening to me during an international conference, said to the person beside him, "That's a real philosophical discourse." Oh, man. . . .

When I got back from Heidelberg I bought my first car. A Fiat 600, naturally. The color of goose shit. Naturally.

12 | "MAD, UTTERLY DESPERATE STUDY"

In 1964 Pareyson shifted to theoretical philosophy, and I took over the course in esthetics. At age twenty-eight I was one of the youngest lecturers in the whole Italian university system.

In 1967 my book *Ipotesi su Nietzsche* (Hypothesis on Nietzsche) came out; I was dumped by a girl I was very seriously engaged to; Palazzo Campana, the heart of the University of Turin, was occupied at the end of November, and I was initially unsure what to think about the student movement; Michele Pellegrino became archbishop of Turin and this had a picaresque impact on my public/private life (it led me one night to the Valentino, the park along the Po where a lot of homosexuals cruise, and from there into the police files); and I suffered a devastating ulcer.

Of both my doubts about the student protest movement—based partly on Pasolinian antibourgeoisism, partly on what Lukács would call romantic anticapitalism—and my ulcer, which wasn't a minor illness back then, I was cured within a few months. Between March and July 1968 I had my own personal '68. As for being in the police files, I don't suppose I was ever cured of that; it's generally a chronic malady.

In fact, I had always worked like crazy ever since I was eighteen. This is no doubt the (very proletarian) reason—along with the way I had lived my homosexuality until then—for the ulcer that plagued me for several years.

During the months when I wasn't at Heidelberg, but also before going there and after coming back, I worked like a beast. I had to work. I was a real proletarian. Private lessons were no longer enough. Mornings I taught children in a state-recognized school run by the Rosminians, three afternoons a week I held office hours at the institute of esthetics—I had rapidly become assistant to Pareyson, but only on contract, which had to be renewed every year and paid a pittance—and the other afternoons I devoted to my book on Heidegger.

Another cause of my ulcer was certainly the *Enciclopedia filosofica,* a doorstop in six volumes that is still around, edited by the Centro Studi Filosofici in Gallarate in collaboration with another Catholic center at Padua. Pareyson was in charge of the historical section, and I worked with him. I'll never forget the long argument about who was going to handle the entry on "God." Was "God" a historical entry or a theoretical entry? In the end it was the Padua crowd who won out. God was a theoretical entry.

13 | VAMPIRES

"Is someone here a vampire? How sure are we that nobody in this lecture hall is a vampire?" I often put this question to my classes as soon as I walk in.

Because, has there ever been a scientific experiment demonstrating that vampires don't exist? No. The moment never came when someone explained once and for all that vampires don't exist. At a certain point, we simply forgot it. We don't bother with it anymore; it doesn't worry us. That problem went out of fashion.

This is an example of "historical paradigm." There are epochs in which people really believe that there are witches and that they should be burned, and they don't end when it's scientifically proved that witches don't exist. We stop believing in them, that's all.

It's the same as what Thomas Kuhn, the American philosopher of science, writes in *The Structure of Scientific Revolutions*. He maintains and explains how science can only proceed within certain frameworks of assumption. Therefore there is no real continuity or cumulativity in science, exactly the way there is no cumulativity in time and history for Heidegger.

Jacques Derrida even thinks that history does not exist. So does Emmanuel Levinas, come to that.

Different paradigms. Occurrences. Flashes.

14 | PARADIGMS

It's the end of metaphysics and the end of Thomism, but it's also the swansong of positivism: truth cannot be the objective mirroring of factual data.

Already in *Being and Time*—and this is one of the fundamental keys to my understanding of Heidegger—he no longer believed in truth as conformity and correspondence. The scholastics had defined truth as the intellect in conformity to the thing. There's the rub. If the world has shrunk to the results of scientific experimentation, then the real world is no more. If true Being is only what can be planned and calculated, then all the rest—sentiments, fears, loves—is just rubbish, stuff to throw away.

So the idea of truth as correspondence between affirmation and factual datum evaporates. Heidegger took this very much to heart. He is a fierce enemy of objectivity, because if the only true rationality is that of the positive sciences, the being of mankind—which he calls *Dasein,* that is, being in the world—becomes impossible to formulate in rational terms.

Is this threatening? Of course not. Where is it that scientists demonstrate the truth of their assertions? Within the community of scientists. If you adduce a theory from quantum physics, it is meaningless to me. First I have to learn the paradigm. Somehow or other I have to be initiated into this science, become a member,

VOCAB

so to speak, of the confraternity. What does that have to do with objective knowledge valid for everyone at all times?

Everything comes about in history. No idea emerges independently of the historical moment.

In recent years I have stated this in all sorts of places, and nobody is scandalized any more. Fiat arose at the end of the nineteenth century, and so did the Ford Motor Company. Frederick Taylor, the Chicago engineer, wrote his book in 1907. The First World War was the first great war of materiel, which forced Western societies to become superorganized for production. It wasn't an accident that Kuhn published his book in 1962. What was happening in America in 1962? The Vietnam War. Scientists were beginning to realize that they were doing science at the bidding of a society that was paying for their experiments. The point is the same: don't imagine that what we are doing is searching for absolute truth; we are trying to understand certain things that are subservient to certain others.

Why on earth does Heidegger—the son of a sexton, someone who throughout the 1910s and into the early 1920s lived at Freiburg cultivating Bible studies and devoting himself to Saint Paul—start to turn against Saint Augustine? Because Saint Augustine introduced too much Greek philosophy into Christianity, he says. And why did he dislike that? Because he disliked the idea of Being as a spectacle that one might regard: Plato, ultimately.

In those years culture and philosophy were animated by revolt against the world Charlie Chaplin depicted in *Modern Times,* even though the film itself belongs to the 1930s. What is it they were against, these philosophers—Karl Jaspers, Karl Barth, Heidegger himself, early existentialism, even in part, and a lot earlier, Søren

Kierkegaard? Against the idea that the dominant strain of Western philosophy had proceeded, from Plato to the positivists, as the unfolding of an idea of truth as objectivity, measurable and demonstrable. For the positivists the only truth was the scientific experiment. Positivistic philosophy served to organize society in a total, and so totalitarian, manner. Positivism was a murderous attack on ethics and liberty. And it had totalitarian society as its inevitable outcome.

I would add one more thing: Heidegger's thought can also be read as a critique of the epoch from a fundamentally political perspective. His thought was driven principally by a refusal of scientific objectivism, not because it was untrue but because it was unjust.

Richard Rorty—whom I got to know a few years later—writes in one of his books that there are, as it were, two lines of modern thought, one Kantian and one Hegelian. The Kantian line seeks the conditions of truth always and everywhere; the Hegelian line seeks truth in the occurrence of Being in history.

If we take the view that Kant is right, or at any rate that there are eternal truths, then we also have to take the view that Aristotle and Plato were stupider than Heidegger, or even than Kant himself, because if truth is just there instead of coming about, then why didn't they already see it? It makes more sense to assume, not that Heidegger was cleverer and more intelligent than Plato, but that Plato was living in a different constellation of Being.

Everything changes. The notion of truth changes. Naturally, the adepts of pure scientism bristle with anger. "What? Science is only valid in such and such a context?" Well, yes indeed, it is only valid in such and such a context.

But that is not as disorienting as it may seem; it doesn't mean we float off into total relativism. Science sheds enough light to allow us to judge whether a proposition is false or not. When something is affirmed, the paradigm for verifying it is also adduced, the coordinates within which that affirmation is true or false are given.

And as far as vampires go, there are criteria for distinguishing the vampires from the nonvampires.

I well remember July 14, 1948, because my sister was on vacation in Cetraro the day Antonio Pallante opened fire on Palmiro Togliatti. Disturbances at Rome, deaths at Naples, Livorno, Genoa.

Here in Turin a group of workers held Vittorio Valletta, the CEO of Fiat, prisoner in his office. The army was getting ready to step in. The next day, June 15, the telephones weren't working and the trains weren't moving. Italy was split in two at Bologna. Then De Gasperi and Pope Pius XII telephoned the Italian cycling team competing in the Tour de France. Gino Bartali was twenty-two minutes behind the yellow jersey, but in the mountains that day he broke away from the field and went on to win the Tour. A huge demonstration planned for five-thirty in the afternoon in Piazza Duomo at Milan was transformed—when the radio announced that Bartali had won—into a huge national festival. Everyone was talking about Bartali. Togliatti and the revolution could wait. I began to understand vaguely what sort of country I was living in.

The postwar period was in full swing. We lived in Via Don Bosco, in a small building right above the offices of the Partito d'Azione. We had succeeded in getting them to let the third floor to us, underneath were the offices, the bar, in sum the clubhouse of the Partito d'Azione. My sister was employed there. She "carried Ferruccio Parri about on her shoulders," she used to say, meaning that she attended demonstrations carrying the placard of the party. The Partito d'Azione, of course, lasted about one day. Having studied accounting a bit and being a good typist, she went to work in one of those businesses that aren't around any more, firms that provided security for rail transport. Later she worked in a less shady place, a shipping agency.

The apartment in Via Don Bosco was small. We found another, bigger one in Via Carlo Alberto, facing Palazzo Campana, the historic seat of the faculties of law, education, and letters and philosophy, where I would later attend university and become a professor, and president of that last faculty.

I read Jack London and wrote my first and only novel, sixty single-space typewritten pages. I didn't yet have my own typewriter; my sister got someone to lend me one. It was the story, set in a mythical Cetraro of course, of two boys who set about making a model airplane. I had already published a poem at my own expense in an unlikely anthology from the publisher Gastaldi called *Poeti italiani per l'amore e la bontà* (Italian poets for love and goodness).

My novel was supposed to be published in the *Gazzetta dei Piccoli* (Children's gazette), a supplement to the *Gazzetta del Popolo.* This was a liberal paper I read for years in defiance of *La Stampa,* the Agnelli-owned paper. The Marquise Paola Bologna edited the *Gazzetta dei Piccoli,* which aped the *Corriere dei Piccoli.* I was already very enterprising. I had written to her and she had replied, "Come and see me."

The building in Corso Valdocco also housed the editorial offices and printing works of the Communist Party newspaper,

L'Unità. Those were the first newspapers that I saw and sniffed close up.

At our meeting the marquise promised to publish my novel. But two weeks later her paper closed, and I joined the countless ranks of unpublished writers.

16 | ORATORY

I am the scion of institutions. Religious ones in my case. Religious corporations educated me.

My father died when I was barely sixteen months old. My aunt was already living on her own, my mother worked all day, my sister likewise. I studied and lived in the street. At this point the "De Gasperi" sisters stepped in, two women who owned a small grocery nearby, at the corner of Via Maria Vittoria and Via Bogino. They got their nickname because they were ultra-Catholic. "Why doesn't this boy go to the oratory?"

So I began to frequent the oratory of San Filippo Neri next door to us, from the courtyard of which you could see the windows of Palazzo Campana. Not out of faith, but for the playmates and the games. Yet it was a decisive passage in my life.

I've always been a group animal, a gregarious animal, albeit with my own individual profile. I was useless at soccer, but I became one of the leaders of Azione Cattolica (Catholic Action) in Turin. In those years and in that setting I met and became friends with Furio Colombo.

Community living gives you many stimuli, but mostly superficial ones. It's true, though, that the "sexual problem," as Sandro Penna calls it, was largely "muffled" in those years at the oratory. Well, not largely. A little.

I was a little saint. Mass every morning, with the main problem being to get to confession the evening before if you had committed "impure acts," so that you could take communion the next day.

And on Saturday afternoon, parties for young teens at the homes of well-off schoolgirls. We boys had to bring the pastries. And often I hadn't enough money. We discovered a place that sold pastries at a discount. God knows what was in them.

I felt liked, however. There was one priest in particular who helped me in all kinds of ways. No money for a school trip? He gave it to me. I read and studied. Snacked on bread, butter, and marmalade. Before long I would abandon Jack London for Thomas Mann. *The Magic Mountain,* but *Death in Venice* as well.

17 | CATHOLIC ACTION

So there you have my Catholic roots. In 1954, when I finished high school, I was already the diocesan student delegate.

It was summertime, and I had finished high school with excellent results. I set out for the Falzarego Pass with a group of Catholic students, of whom I was the leader, for ten days of school camp at one of the numerous former fascist youth organization colonies, some of which had been handed over to the Communists and others to the Catholics. A fine band of individuals, some smarter than me. Like Michele Straniero, for example.

And there we started a *fronde*. We used the evening transmission over the camp radio to advertise "Clerodont toothpaste. Anticurial, the toothpaste of the clerical hierarchy." Bad jokes, really, but they hit the mark because they derided the new national presidency of the Catholic youth association ferociously. After three days they sent all of us from Turin home, seventeen individuals out of 150. I don't have to tell you how proud we were of having been chased out.

After they threw us out of Azione Cattolica, too, in 1955, Michele Straniero and I and a number of others—including Franco Bolgiani and Eugenio Corsini, who were already university lecturers—founded the Mounier Group.

That's the background against which I began to read Mounier.

Emmanuel Mounier had invented what in Italy was called the "community movement," a communitarianism that was also a way of multiplying society's intermediate bodies: the family, the neighborhood community, the cooperative. The periodical *Terza Generazione* was being published at this time by Bartolo Ciccardini and Gianni Baget Bozzo, and to some extent also by Augusto Del Noce, although he didn't actually write for it. It lasted only a year, but Elio Vittorini was greatly intrigued by it, and Natalia Ginzburg published there at least once. And the *Terza Generazione* group, who lived between Turin and Moncalieri, had formed consumer cooperatives modeled on Mounier's communitarianism.

I had taken a few ideas from that journal for my final high-school essay, the usual thing: there is Soviet communism and there is liberal capitalism, but we are different from either.

In sum, Azione Cattolica was a lively place at that time. The struggle between the progressives and the conservatives was fierce: Luigi Gedda versus Carlo Carretto (who later became Brother Carlo in the monastery at Spello, near Perugia), Carretto versus Gedda. . . .

At a certain point Carlo Carretto, the national president, was replaced by Mario Rossi, who seemed to be readier to accept discipline. In fact, he soon went over to the "bad guys" (that is, us). The next national president was entirely reliable. He was called Enrico Vinci, and he was so reliable that nobody has heard of him for a long time.

Another member of Azione Cattolica nationally at that time was Don Arturo Paoli, who later became a "little brother" in Brazil, the author of some really beautiful books. I was tremendously moved the day he came to visit me at home in the afternoon, while I was studying. All he said was, "I was passing by."

I saw him last year, a combative ninety-three-year-old.

18 | BEYOND THE HORIZON

I've already mentioned my eternal need to work. Study and work. To pay the bills, not because of ideology; I wasn't yet acquainted with Mao's little red book.

That summer, the summer of 1954, the summer I graduated from high school, I was at the point of going to work for Generali, the insurance company. I had filled out an application because I needed a job. I consoled myself with the thought that Kafka too had worked for Assicurazioni Generali. In the worst case, I told myself, that's a great example.

During those months the RAI—which had started to transmit on January 3, the day before my eighteenth birthday—had been occupied by Catholics, progressive Catholics of that era, luckily, followers of Giorgio La Pira: *cattocommunisti* (Catholic communists) before the word existed.

In June, Filiberto Guala was named CEO. He was Turinese, a Catholic engineer, but who came from the FUCI, the progressive Italian Catholic university association, and had also worked at RIV, a branch of Fiat. He was highly efficient, and had been Fanfani's point man for the INA Casa plan for housing—in other words, one of the few serious undertakings in postwar Italy. The first thing Guala did was to hold a public competition for employees; he was looking for staff. He met the handful of winners and realized immediately that he didn't know what to do with them. A few came from journalism, mostly the fascist kind, but many were young actors with trained voices.

I remember them, my comrades: Ezio Zefferi, Paolino Rosi, and Tito Stagno, beautiful as the sun, Carlo Mazzarella, who arched his feet when he walked so he would look taller.

Guala thought: how am I going to launch the new television medium with human material like this? Simpatico and clever they may be, but still. . . .

So he started going around to the Catholic associations looking for someone, anyone, to give him a hand. He came to Turin and was told about Umberto Eco, Furio Colombo, and myself. Umberto was a national director of Azione Cattolica's youth wing, a friend of Mario Rossi. I was a youth barely out of high school; they had already finished university.

In 1954 Guala hired us on a grant: 65,000 lire (the lira of the 1950s; it would amount to a few hundred euros or dollars today).

First we all did a three-month course, September to December, in Milan. We had to learn how to do everything: newscaster, host, functionary. When the three months were up, Furio and Umberto stayed in Milan and I went back to Turin: I wanted to go back home so I could live with my mother. I didn't like living away, I was enrolled in university, I wanted to study as well as work.

But it was really fun, there were some unique characters: I recall Pier Emilio Gennarini, a super-integrist super-Catholic, but with a leftward twist, sort of a Romano Prodi fifty years in advance.

In Milan I had a really great time. I lived with Furio and Umberto, and in the evenings, when they didn't drag me off to Santa Tecla—a den of perversity, they played jazz there and you could meet girls, which greatly worried my spiritual director, Monsignor Caramello—we stayed home and Umberto explained medieval philosophy to me, because I had an upcoming examination on that: Eloise and Abelard and so on.

In January 1955 I started working for the RAI in Turin. Everything was clustered together: the office, the university, my home.

I did a weekly program for young people directed by Furio, with Umberto as a consultant of sorts. Furio—what can one say? Even then he was the type who forced his team to really commit, I believe he ran *L'Unità* the same way, long editorial meetings . . .

The program was called *Orrizonte*. It was broadcast in the afternoon, at 6:00 PM, when the kids were still up. For a while nobody took any notice, they were all watching the evening news.

I interviewed Danilo Dolci not long before he went to occupy land in Sicily, and he announced on our program that he was going to do so.

Dario Fo and Giustino Durano also came on *Orrizonte*. Durano invited me to go on tour with him; he had created a revue company. He said to me, "You're good, forget about the RAI."

Michele Straniero and I invented a segment of *Orrizonte* called "Controviaggio in Italia" (at that time there was a radio program called *Viaggio in Italia* with Guido Piovene). The idea was to go around to Italian cities and do real, disturbing investigative journalism with help from young people who had organized themselves, from youth associations, from unions. We did two shows, from Asti and Piacenza, but when we got to La Spezia for the third we focused on the arms manufacturer Oto Melara, and therefore the problem of military procurement . . . and they shut us down on the spot. Just before we went on air there was a general rehearsal, which the head honchos in Rome could watch on a low-frequency channel. They immediately telephoned Susanna Egri, a great ballerina from Turin who had her own program in which she taught basic dancing. She was the one they always kept ready to go on the air in case there was a sudden "hole" in the schedule for political reasons.

Meantime I had to keep studying. There was an exam to prepare for on Kant's *Critique of Judgment,* of which I understood absolutely nothing, not even the commas, a real disaster.

Guala was too free a spirit and was forced to resign by a genuine conspiracy between the Christian Democrats and the Vatican. He resigned on June 18, 1956. After a spell back at INA Casa, he became a Trappist monk at age fifty-three in the Frattocchie convent and was ordained as a priest in 1967.

Guala had always given us plenty of protection; with him out of the way, Marcello Rodinò arrived and everything changed. Rodinò was passionate about sailing. And not much else.

But for a couple of years the RAI in Turin had been a gathering point, a place for doing new things, for debating freely. A large slice of the Turinese intelligentsia took part: Luciano Gallino, Paolo Siniscalco, Vincenzo Incisa, Folco Portinari. From a little farther off, Emanuele Milano.

At that time I got to know Walter Bonatti, and we remained friends; we've even gone climbing together.

But I was getting tired and feeling cramped in that milieu. In 1957 I quit, and Monsignor Caramello found me a job as a teacher in the Casa di Carità Arti e Mestieri, a charitable vocational and trade school.

19 | WORKING-CLASS SCHOOL

So I dropped the RAI and went to teach in the Casa di Carità Arti e Mestieri, an interagency school run by the Unione Catechisti del Santissimo Crocifisso (Catechistic Union of the Holiest Cross) and by Maria Santissima Immacolata, a suborder of the Fratelli delle Scuole Cristiane (Brothers of the Christian Schools) that served the working classes, in the sense that they taught trades. But there was a cultural component. I taught culture, religion, and civics.

The kids who attended the school were from the working-class outskirts, Michelin workers mostly.

I studied Thomas Aquinas and prepared religion lectures on that. For the "culture" component, I started with a normal survey text, but then I gave them the *Apology of Socrates* and one or two other things by Plato to read. Civics was important to me, and I taught it straight from the Italian constitution.

At a certain point the friars told me they couldn't keep me on and got rid of me: I was seen as a dangerous subversive.

So I got a job teaching with the Rosminians, in lower middle school where I couldn't do any harm: all I had to do was explain the rules of Latin, history, Italian, geography. . . . I stayed there three years, teaching the same kids in first, second, and third grade.

As a prole myself, I suppose I had the campaign for literacy in the blood, because ten years later, during the protest movement, when groups and small parties like the PSIUP (the party of "proletarian unity") were forming to the left of the Communist Party, I used to spend my evenings helping youths get their intermediate certificate. We used to go out to the sections of the PSIUP bunch who had got it into their heads to give literacy courses in the outskirts, at Le Vallette.

A very exciting period. I was already getting a real thrill from the boys, but naturally I kept that clamped down.

You see, these particular boys were really incredible. They turned up in the evening to study, and then on Saturday afternoon, instead of just hanging out, they came back and we taught them to understand classical music. Vittorio Rieser, who is in fact an excellent pianist, played and explained Mozart. It was always full.

Those boys, I remember every one of them, I dream about them at night. There was one boy from Friuli, beautiful and blond, named Lino Faccin. I liked him tremendously. Once he wrote in an essay, "And then the evening came, this joyous avant-garde of night." I sat there stunned. It sounded like Shakespeare . . . and maybe it was. I still wonder if he wrote it himself. Nor am I certain he was really the author of these words from his essay on "My life as a Worker," but they are no less moving for that: "Monday morning I get up at six, and I am so nervous I don't speak a word."

20 | DEMONIC POSSESSION

Why did the Fratelli delle Scuole Cristiane decide to get rid of me when I was twenty-three? Because I had started to frequent trade unionists, take part in worker strikes, picket factory gates. I picketed with the guys from the labor organization CISL at the Avigliana ironworks, for example.

One day there was a demonstration in front of the prefecture, nothing controversial, it was against apartheid in South Africa, but there was a bit of commotion. The police blew the thing up, calling it an assault on the prefecture. Apparently someone on our side had proposed that we charge the barrier of policemen, who were decked out in military gear. To give you an idea of what things were like then.

At Turin there was a trade union fringe, not *Quaderni Rossi* exactly, but close: Pino Ferraris, Clemente Ramella, Giulia Bissaca, Tommaso Musolini, PSIUP types, left-wing extremists. I was with them. We founded a Documentation Center, as the fashion then was. I knew English, so I took on the job of translating IRA documents. I don't know whether I ever translated handbooks for making bombs, I don't think so, I would have remembered. . . .

The key episode for me occurred in 1959. The national metalworkers' contract was up for renewal, and tension was high. There was a very bitter strike at RIV, a Fiat branch at Lingotto, in Via Nizza.

The usual gigantic phalanx of cops.

I was there picketing with many others, a few guys who later joined Rainero Panzieri's *Quaderni Rossi:* Vittorio Rieser, Giovanni Mottura. I was waving my copy of the constitution. We were trying to keep the scabs from getting in. There were a lot of us. I remember even seeing the head of the local Boy Scouts.

All of a sudden the cops charged, threw us into a wagon, and took us to police headquarters. The matter was cleared up in a few hours, but I was assistant professor to Pareyson, I had the keys to the institute of esthetics, I had to go and open up. . . . As soon as they let me go I rushed to phone the master, out of breath. "I've had some trouble, sorry."

Next day the headline on the front page of *L'Unità* read, "Young Catholic manager arrested in front of RIV while reciting verses from the gospel." On the same page Giancarlo Pajetta awarded me an honorary membership card in the FGCI, the Communist youth organization.

My mother saved that front page from *L'Unità,* but I can't find it now.

I was starting to become a public personality, someone serious about what he was doing, and also fodder for the newspapers.

Michele Straniero told me that *Studi cattolici* (a periodical that is still being published, linked to Opus Dei) wrote that I had been possessed by the devil. I was supposed to have been overcome with fever, been in the hospital, and come out a "convert" to communism.

21 | ULCER AND MAO

The ulcer began in Germany, and it gradually got worse. A bleeding ulcer. Early in 1968, while I was at a philosophical convention in Rome, I had to go to bed and stay there, immobile, for two weeks. What could I do? Be patient and read.

Back in Turin I was admitted to hospital, at the Molinette. They operated.

Away from the university and the daily grind I relaxed a bit, began to unwind.

I left the hospital and convalesced at San Remo with my mother, my brother-in-law, and my sister.

I read continually, stuff I hadn't had time or opportunity to read before. I read Herbert Marcuse's *Eros and Civilization,* and especially *Soviet Marxism,* in French because they weren't yet out in Italian.

On March 13, 1968 (unforgettable), I woke up a Maoist. I drafted a note I still have around here somewhere entitled "Why Mao." Period.

For me everything was changing: politics, private life. Everything.

As for *Studi cattolici* . . . they weren't so far off the mark after all.

22 | THE DREAM OF A THING

Who can ever recount summer afternoons, the lassitude and the languor of certain summer Sundays? Nothing else is so close to the surface of the skin, alive and desperate at the same time.

There was a boy who was my colleague at the Casa di Carità, a swimming champion, beautiful as an angel, strong. I passed tormenting Sundays with him, reading him *The Good Person of Sichuan*.

One afternoon I said to him, "Let's go rowing on the Po." We got on a bus. There was just me, him, and a mother with a young daughter who looked a bit retarded, watching us with a dribble of spit coming out of her mouth . . . she was looking at us the way I was looking at my friend.

When I started to frequent cruising places . . . it was even worse. I remember terrifying afternoons, with springtime in the blood, the eyes, the nerves . . . restless as a cat . . . without finding anyone, in the end.

Or leaving the house on foot to go to the Valentino Park, then waiting for the last tram.

I don't often feel self-pity, on the contrary. But sometimes I felt like a bit of a sorry figure then. And sorry about Don Pietro.

Certain summer afternoons I would go to his place and find him with a few buttons of his black suit undone, and the air of someone who had undergone terrible carnal temptations, his features haggard, unshaven.

But there wasn't only torment.

In mid-August there's this sense of emptiness, it's true, but also of great freedom, this sensation of living a moment out of the ordinary. A bit like during a general strike: every stranger you meet is a friend. And you converse, without effort, with tranquil complicity, with naturalness, with the awareness of sharing a completely extraordinary situation.

At Heidelberg, the first year, I worked extremely hard on my Heidegger book. It was a great intellectual adventure, but a physical one too, an exhausting labor. I remember the most beautiful summer back in Turin, a bit Pasolinian. I would work all day and then walk around at night, searching, but without that desperation. The feeling was more like a buzz, the reward you give yourself, the breath you draw till your lungs are full after a tiring day, but one well spent and full of satisfaction.

23 | TAKE A KING AND THRASH HIM

The first great loves have also been examples for me as well. All the unconsummated ones, I mean.

Between the fourth and fifth grades in middle school, I desperately desired a classmate named Renzo. I went to Rome with him during the holy year in 1950. We were fourteen. We slept at Santa Maria where the cardinals live now, in cots separated by curtains. We talked all night, telling each other we were in love with the same little girl, but male friendship came first, so it was "I leave her to you." "No, I leave her to *you*."

In fact, it was him I wanted. The thought of kissing him all over drove me crazy. I suffered the torments of inferno. I admired him a lot too; he was beautiful, rich, good at sports; he could jump higher than me. I saw him recently and I said to him, "Do you realize I have always been in love with you?" And he said, "No, I've never had that problem." What kind of answer is that? I've never understood it. Who knows, maybe if I had been more daring it would have been a great love.

Alberto was a great climber; he later became a director of the Italian Alpine Club.

He had a beautiful Moto Guzzi on which we used to go to monarchist meetings singing a song in dialect, "*Prendere un re e bastonarlo*" (Take a king and thrash him). We would glide through these meetings singing and then take off, because otherwise they would have beaten us up.

I went to the mountains with him, to the shelter at Grandes Jorasses. Him I *was* tempted to seduce, we two were alone there, beneath the Jorasses. I had brought Aristotle's *Poetics* because I was working on my thesis, and Alberto had a little book of Leopardi's poetry, one of those little pocket editions. There were mice running around at night, I could easily have jumped into bed with him from fear. I never had the courage to do it.

He joked about it, called me Tadzio, the beautiful boy from *Death in Venice*. Why? I don't know, never will.

I tried once with Sergio, also in the mountains, also without getting anywhere, one night when we were sleeping in the same sleeping bag.

Sergio and Alberto . . . I call them my two friends stronger than me. They were really presences, I don't know how else to put it.

One night when a hustler threatened to blackmail me, taking down my license plate and saying he was going to phone me at home, it was those two I called. Right away they said: let's go find that son of a bitch and beat him black and blue, the bastard.

24 | PORTA PALAZZO

I've never taken myself too seriously. And—Sergio always criticized me for this—I've never had a particular predilection for details, and so never taken much care over them. I haven't kept a diary. I envy Alessandro Galante Garrone, whose biography I read recently. He always wrote everything down, day by day, minute by minute. A great historian, of himself too. Not me. I don't even have a complete archive of the things I have written, or that others have written about me. Now that my students Mario Cedrini, Alberto Martinengo, and Santiago Zabala are organizing the publication of my collected works, they are going to have their hands full.

In the mind, many dates get mixed up. And time dilates or contracts in memory.

But I remember perfectly every detail of the first time I went looking for a hustler.

I had been at the Olivetti factory, summoned by Furio Colombo, who worked there and insisted I should come for an interview too. So I went along to be inspected by the managers: Nicola Tufarelli, and then Carlo Novara, whom I still see at demonstrations, at that time head psychologist for Olivetti. Neither had much enthusiasm for me. I don't suppose I made much of an impression on these Olivetti types, and anyway I wanted to study philosophy.

I had taken the bus to Ivrea. On the way back, I remembered Porta Palazzo. One of the boys I met in Azione Cattolica had told me about it, without suspecting my interest: "If you go to Porta Palazzo, you can find guys who prostitute themselves." Porta Palazzo has always been where you go to find everything, for that matter.

I got off the bus and went to Porta Palazzo, the corner of Via XX Settembre and Corso Regina. There was still rubble there from the bombings, and the dirty business was carried on amid the rubble. I had never seen a hustler in my life. I saw this boy leaning against a pole. Naturally he wanted to be paid first, but I had no money in my pockets. We talked a bit. He told me his name was Marcello. Up came an old man who explicitly wanted me. I was a good-looking blond boy too, then. Marcello started urging me, "Come on, go for it, make some money." But I just didn't want to, and finally I left and went home.

But one evening, after leaving *La Stampa*, where I had gone looking for archival material that Furio had asked me for, I went back, trying to walk unobtrusively. And there I found him, just the same, thin as a rail, the same Marcello. We went to a park, the Giardini Reali. I could still show you the tower we went to the base of. It was the evening before Epiphany, January 5, 1961. That's how I celebrated my twenty-fifth birthday, just one day late.

The devastating feeling of guilt afterward—I needn't tell you.

But I've also had occasion to act in defense of the oppressed. The shining, fearless hero.

In June 1967, Michele Pellegrino was named cardinal by Pope Paul VI and became the archbishop of Turin, so his chair at the university fell vacant.

One evening I went to see Pareyson to talk about this critical juncture for us and the city. On my way home in my car, I decided to drive by the Valentino Park. I'm driving along slowly, looking around, and at a certain point I see a group of cops ganging up on a thin little rent boy, giving him a beating. Without thinking, I stop my car, get out, identify myself, and take up the kid's defense until they let him go. But the cops aren't too happy about being interrupted, and they take it out on me. I'm a reputable university teacher, so there's only so much they can do to me. But precisely the fact that I'm a reputable professor makes me vulnerable. Their questions were more than insinuating: "And you sir, what are you doing here at this hour?" "I was passing through, on my way home." And that's how I got into the police files.

25 | FROM HEIDEGGER TO MARX

This may seem incredible, but if you work through Heidegger you can easily get to Marx. Heidegger's forgetting of Being can be likened to Marx's alienation and Lukács's reification. In at least two ways: you can't change anything by yourself, so to sort things out you have to make a revolution; and the forgetting of Being as Heidegger thinks it is what Marxism explains with the division of labor: you yourself don't enjoy all the fruits of your labor, and a society is erected in which everything is commodified, including you as a worker.

When Heidegger says that there is not principally man but Being, and we reply, Being thinks itself in us, well, that's Marx: there's no use exerting yourself trying to be different if society doesn't change. Marx imagines you can do it by taking the Winter Palace. Okay, but slow down. In order to take the Winter Palace, a quantity of conditions have to be realized, which it isn't that far-fetched to call Heidegger's Being. There needs to be a great transformation.

When we were young and the priests would tell us that making the revolution meant, above all, achieving self-renewal, what they obviously meant was: you can be authentic no matter what your life situation is—in fact, just be an onlooker and leave things as they are. Don't bother with politics, with rich and poor; go to church and meditate and save your soul.

Well, sorry, my friends, but no. That won't cut it.

Becoming a Maoist (I say this half in jest and half seriously), discovering that as a Heideggerian I was also a Hegelian-Marxist, didn't make me a convert to the student movement overnight. Far from it.

My stance as an anticapitalist romantic made me think: the capitalist world is a big rubbish heap, but these people here, these well-bred students, will never change anything, much less make the revolution.

And to be honest, the slogans that got them worked up made me laugh. For example: "We want university departments, not institutes." Laugh? No, that was really stupid. Okay, the institutes were based on single professorial chairs, meaning that someone like Pareyson had a room, a library, and the money to keep the show going. The students wanted departments instead because departments consisted of all the professors running things jointly. Well, you know . . . "department" was fundamentally an American term. It was hard for me not to agree with Pareyson during our long debates, when he would say, needling me for my anticapitalist Heideggerism, "We are much more revolutionary than that lot, all they want is to change a few university structures, we are people absolutely outside the organicity of this situation. I prefer a traditional university to a more functional, modern university run like

Fiat." That was convincing to someone like me who had always been against modernity and the oppressive functioning of positivist capitalism.

I have to admit, though, that when I was wearing two hats myself, as a professor and a revolutionary, I found myself pulled both ways. But I participated in the assemblies and the processions, and I used to tell the ultra-Catholic Pareyson: "Professor, why don't you come to the demonstration too, look, it's like going to church, everyone calls everyone else comrade, there's a real feeling of coming together for justice." And he would reply, "You must be kidding. I don't want to wind up like the mayor of Peking"—whom the Red Guards had paraded around wearing donkey ears.

The situation was embarrassing, and not just from the intellectual point of view but in practical terms too. Picture a packed hall, with students shouting "Gianni Gianni sei tutti noi" (Gianni, Gianni, you are all of us), and there I am, president of my faculty, standing on the podium beside the rector and the other presidents and coping as best I can. . . . There was Galante Garrone, too; he had been a good partisan in the wartime Resistance, but nobody took the sixties student revolt less seriously than he did.

But before, when the protest movement first exploded, I didn't know. Didn't know the most important thing. That within a few months, in summer, June 1968, my whole life would change. I was about to meet two people who, as well as giving me love for the first time at age thirty-two, would be my true masters, life masters, would make me more free with myself and vis-à-vis others, even freer inside my head, in my work as a thinker, a philosopher.

Between 1968 and 1972 I worked a lot on Nietzsche, studying and taking notes. Then, in twenty days of marvelous madness, in the mountains once more, in the summer of 1972, I wrote *Il soggetto e la maschera* (The subject and the mask). In 1969, the year Adorno died, I had become full professor of esthetics. And I was about to turn another page right after the summer of 1972, because I had been invited to teach in America for the first time.

But for now we're still at the start of the summer of '68.

27 | STATE OF GRACE

When I went into a store with him, it was as if they had opened a skylight.

His name was Julio, and he was a Peruvian dancer. Utterly beautiful, gentle, sharp, and sweet. And very sensual. It was he who taught me that in bed you can, you must, be completely free. It was with him that I experienced passion, love for another person that is also the maximum of desire. It was his smile that first of all and more than anything moved me. When the first thing I do is look someone in the eyes, that's the sign that I am in love.

Today when I say in love, I am saying that I desire beauty, of course, but above all your presence, having you in the house, going to the cinema together, almost more being able to go on a trip together than make love, although lovemaking certainly wouldn't be bad either.

I've always had a hard time making love and sex coincide. For many years, like the Catholics, like Saint Paul, I regarded sex as a pressing need, to be met as quickly as possible. It was my background, I suppose, but also the historical epoch in which I lived. I don't believe I have had a happy sexual life.

I saw Julio for the first time in the house of some acquaintances. I froze. Thunderstruck. Dazed. Madly in love.

When you're in that state, you don't think about anything else.

I had to find him again, but how? Days spent searching for him, tracking him, with little to go on. A dancer. Arrived in London with a Peruvian dance troupe and then bolted to Turin on his own. A dancer. For the first time I said to a few people, my best and oldest friends, Melita and Piero, "I'm in love, I'm in love." "With whom?" "With a Peruvian *ballerino*." "Oh, that's great." Didn't bat an eyelid. A dancer. The theater. They helped me find him. We thought of the university theater center.

He was there.

It was a month . . . you know the kind of thing you feel? When you feel yourself welcome in the eyes of God and man. With Julio it was like that. I felt myself in a state of grace. I kept repeating, incredulous, "I'm in love, I'm in love." I was still living with my mother. Melita and Piero loaned us their place.

Everyone fell at his feet. All around him. Shopgirls, clerks, mothers, grandmothers, aunts and uncles.

He illuminated the world. He was benediction, he was like Jesus.

I had just had an operation for my ulcer and was ashamed of my body. He told me I shouldn't be ashamed of the body, of sex. He really educated me, taught me a new rapport with sex, meaning with myself.

One day we ran into Pareyson in Piazza Castello. Julio had a salmon-pink jacket I had given him the day before. I introduced him to my master with some embarrassment, but not that much.

It only lasted a month and a half. But we always remained friends and kept in touch. I remember when he came to visit me in New York in 1973, and I was living in a house full of cockroaches. We slept in the same bed and waged war on them with boric acid for ammunition.

He suddenly decided to go to Rome, get married, have a daughter. In a small way, I still take care of her.

Abandoned, I thought I would die.

28 | THE BICYCLE LEFT BEHIND

Hegel used to say: decide to get married first, then look for a wife. That's how it was with Gianpiero. A choice. Just as my sister's marriage was a rational choice, following an unhappy grand passion.

If you marry for passion, it ends badly.

Before him, apart from Julio, I had had "friends." But they were those terrifying things I did at night. In hiding. Even from myself.

My heart was in pieces when Julio left.

A friend introduced me to Gianpiero. From then on, until his death, for twenty-four years, we were always together.

He wasn't even twenty, thirteen years younger than me. He came from the sit-in at the Massimo D'Azeglio high school and enrolled in the university.

We were really fond of each other. He was simpatico, intelligent. Utterly sweet. And me with all my doubts, with the fear, or rather the certainty, that I wasn't his type, that I didn't please him enough physically, that I wasn't exactly like the men he desired.

Neither of us ever dreamed for a moment that the other would be "faithful" to him. We even went to saunas together, and inside it was every man for himself, obviously. All the same there were outbursts of jealousy, on his part and mine. Even though he had many more encounters than me. That was always my problem with my friends who were younger than I was: they had many more encounters than I did, and I always felt a bit embarrassed. It isn't that I didn't want to "betray" them. I was that I couldn't.

But we got on so well together. And I still have letters from him in which he writes, "Do whatever you want, the important thing is that our feelings remain." Because he did what he wanted, and then, as now—accepting suffering and contradictions—that seemed to me absolutely just.

But being together was calming for both of us. We had had, like the majority of homosexuals, especially then, difficult lives. His parents found out from his diary that he had had an affair with a friar who was his teacher of religion.

Even in sex we were very reserved, restrained. We were almost like a Christian married couple: "I don't do it for pleasure, only to make children for God." In our case children were out of the question, but you get the idea. I exaggerate a little, but not much.

One of the first memories I have with Gianpiero is that we went to a crummy little movie house to see Pasolini's *Teorema,* which had caused a scandal when it was presented at the Venice Biennale in 1968.

In the early years I still lived with my mother, and when I did leave home, it was to live with Gianpiero. My mother and I had changed apartments twice more, first we were in Via Vassalli Eandi, then in Corso Francia, near Rivoli, a beautiful spot in front of a villa that is still in use as a municipal garden, called Villa Tesoreria.

Gianpiero and I saw each other every day. Often he ate at my house, and then we went out to the cinema. Or else we stayed home with my friends Piero and Melita in Piazza Vittorio.

The first years were really happy. He taught me so much, and freed me from so much. He convinced me to wear a duffel coat of the sort that all the left-wing students then wore, a coat purchased at the Standa department store for ten thousand lire that made me euphoric. It represented the crucial change of my life. The watershed between before and after. I remember that black duffel coat that I wore all winter and made me feel free in the wildest way.

It went on like that until autumn 1972, when I was invited for the first time to teach in the United States. In September I left for New York, and Gianpiero came with me. He stayed for a month and then returned; he had a job as a teacher in an evening school. I got back in the middle of winter, after four months.

And at this point, in the spring of 1973, we decided to move in together. Up on the hill, as we say in Turin, at Valsalice. We found an apartment in a rustic building and fixed it up ourselves, together. It was the start of the happiest period of my life.

We drove down every morning in the Diane and went to the university.

You're too young, Stefano, you wouldn't remember. But there was the oil crisis, the famous pedestrian Sundays. We used to walk down from the hill on foot too, happy as cats.

Cats were something we had plenty of.

A stream ran under the house, I got rheumatism for life, yet it was lovely. There was so much humidity I never heard the newspapers rustle.

And I remember 1974, when a fiercely contested referendum made divorce legal in Italy. We drove into town with the top down and went to celebrate in Via Roma amid a huge crowd, an epic affair, like when Italy won the World Cup.

One day Ezio Mauro, then a young reporter with the *Gazzetta del Popolo,* came round. We talked in the garden and then an article came out with a terrible photo of me, but in *Panorama,* because he also wrote for the weekly.

We always had beautiful vacations, first in Yugoslavia and then in Greece, at Thassos, Ithaca, Santorini.

War and Peace I read only at the start of the 1980s, at Santorini, and it was such a beautiful experience that I was glad I hadn't read it earlier.

At Ithaca, on the other hand, we lodged with a lady we called Nonna Papera (Granny Duck). In the middle of the country, with no electric light, but near an irresistible little beach. Nonna Papera's husband—don't ask me why—lived in a hut in a tree. He stayed there all day and all night.

We went on vacation with Mario and my great friend Angela, a psychoanalyst. That's one of the reasons I still have close ties to Mario, since he has been a widower. They always left two or three days ahead of me because I unfailingly had some job to finish.

I hadn't publicly professed my homosexuality, it wasn't inscribed anywhere officially, but everyone knew I was living with my friend and that gave me a great measure of peace.

Once I got back from a trip abroad and found a racing bicycle left behind in our garage. It wasn't hard to imagine how Gianpiero had entertained himself and passed the time while I was away.

Gianpiero was a Germanist. He studied a great deal of German literature with Claudio Magris. Magris was his master, in a manner of speaking. About *Danube,* Gianpiero used to say, "Yes, interesting . . . it's all cribbed from Baedeker."

So Gianpiero was headed for a brilliant career as a Germanist.

At Easter in 1969 or 1970—I don't recall—we went with two friends of ours, Paola and Giorgio, to Budapest in a car. And we went to visit Gyorgy Lukács. We rang him up, and a maid answered; then he came to the telephone, and I asked him in German if we could pay him a visit. I wasn't yet known outside Italy. Lukács had been here in Turin to give a lecture in the great hall of the university a few years before, but I hadn't met him.

He lived on an upper floor, across from the Chain Bridge with windows on the Danube. I remember that we were waiting for him in the living room, and he arrived carrying a pair of slippers; maybe he had just returned home. He pulled on his slippers in front of us and we began to chat.

I could already speak German fairly well, and Gianpiero very well. I had just given an esthetics course on Ernst Bloch—art and utopia—so I began to discuss Bloch with Lukács, and he said "Yes, yes, Bloch, of course." But the unspoken message seemed to be "Bloch was a great thinker, and above all a poet, but . . . he was a bit of a poseur" (*dava un po' i numeri;* in Piedmontese the verb would be *davanare*). He spoke to us about the book he was writing, *The Ontology of Social Being.*

So Gianpiero began to get passionately interested in Hungarian. He hadn't done his thesis yet. Back in Italy, he began to write his thesis in Hungarian with a professor, Paolo Santarcangeli, a great friend of Leo Valiani, the sort of people with connections to the Partito d'Azione wing of the resistance. Santarcangeli was from Fiume and knew Hungarian because of the Austro-Hungarian Empire. A real personality. Very worldly, very elegant, a bon vivant, rich. He was ninety years old, had been president of the fashion association, had written a book on the voyage to the underworld, and was studying labyrinths.

I am glad, today—it consoles me a little for the uncompletedness that scandalizes me about his life—that Gianpiero was able to frequent personalities like that. Like Santarcangeli. Or like Cesare Cases, who was a great literary scholar, even though he was an Einaudi snob to the core of his being. The Einaudi publishing house had the rights to the works of Nietzsche but always refused to publish him. It came to the point that when a group from Einaudi left to found the new publishing house Adelphi, the rights went with them.

Through Cases's daughter, who had also become a student of Hungarian, there was this sort of friendship between Cases, Gianpiero, and me.

Gianpiero became associate professor of Hungarian and had a few students, Bruno Ventavoli among them. Gianpiero was one of those who had discovered Sandor Marai. When he died Gianpiero was writing a book on Marai (I still have fragments of it). In Italy, no had ever heard of Marai. Gianpiero also wrote a book on Hungarian Jewish culture, *Fuori dal ghetto,* for Edizioni E/O.

•

He had a lot to teach me about literature. He understood it better than Magris—I'm not impartial, I know, but I am also rationally convinced of this—and without knowing it he was a "weak thinker" in his reading, which challenged Magris, of the German classics. Whereas Magris, for example, warmed to the young Hofmannsthal's *Letter of Lord Chandos,* Gianpiero read Hofmannsthal as an instance of the so-called Potemkin effect, after the prince of Crimea who painted poverty and desolation over with picturesque village facades when Empress Catherine II came to visit.

In 1976 we decided to look for a house in Turin, and I found an attic in Via Mazzini, a beautiful place, in the same building in which Felice Casorati had had his studio in the 1930s. There was a sort of little house that divided the courtyard in two, and it was there that Casorati had lived and worked.

By now we lived with just one cat, because we were unable to bring them all into town. In any case they were used to being outdoors and had never seen a litter box. But abandoning them was a tremendous wrench.

One of the things for which I can't forgive myself is that I didn't bring Carpaccio into town. Carpaccio was a lazy plump little cat. He looked like Garfield. A glutton, colored off-white. He wasn't a beautiful cat, but he was unusually affectionate, and we called him Carpaccio because he looked like one of those animals, a bit shapeless, that you see on the floor at the bottom of Carpaccio's paintings.

We abandoned him the morning we moved house. When he saw the movers arriving to take the furniture away he bolted, and when he came back there was nobody there any more. I hope cats don't have long memories.

More than once I've gone by our old house, making cat noises and calling him to see if he might pop into view. But he didn't trust our car any more.

I hit forty in 1976. It was the year Heidegger died (I had just edited and translated a collection of his essays and speeches). It was the year Gianpiero and I decided to abandon beautiful but inconvenient Valsalice and come back into town to live, so I was looking for an apartment. And it was the year of the national elections.

Not just any elections. The eighteen-year-olds were voting for the first time, and after the clamorous defeat of the moderates in the divorce referendum of 1974 and the debacle of the Christian Democrats in the local elections of 1975, many expected the Italian Communist Party to overtake them (which actually happened, like a will-o-the-wisp, eight years later in the European elections of 1984, when Enrico Berlinguer died at Padua).

In 1976, the Radical Party campaigned in an election for the first time. Women headed all their slates—I don't remember this, but Angelo Pezzana, who is Turinese, records it in his autobiography—and every slate had at least one homosexual candidate, because "Fuori" (the acronym is the Italian word for "out"), which Pezzana founded, took part under the Radical Party umbrella.

One morning I walk into the faculty council and I see everyone with their heads buried in a newspaper. Then they look at me.

So I look at the paper and see this headline: "Vattimo running for Fuori." Uh-oh. Panic.

They hadn't even asked me beforehand. They hadn't even told me afterward. I found out I was a candidate in the elections, and a homosexual candidate at that, from the papers. Perhaps if they had asked me first I wouldn't have accepted, but by now it was done. There it was in writing. It was official.

My first concern was to hide the newspaper from my mother, whom I had never told I was gay. It was my sister who made sure she didn't see it.

The rest I had to deal with myself. I thought: Pareyson will never look me in the eye again, no one will ever invite me to lecture again, I'll always be a homosexual philosopher and not a philosopher. Instead, I actually became faculty president not long after. Partly by chance (the designated candidate suddenly withdrew the evening before), but the fact is, they did elect me.

I got some anonymous letters, it's true; one was even in verse, and I knew immediately who had sent it. It came from a young colleague. The typescript had exactly the same typing mistakes I had always observed in the articles this colleague sent me for the *Rivista di estetica*. I never said anything to him, but I told others, who must certainly have let him know I knew.

Apart from that, none of my fears were realized. On the contrary.

Gianpiero was more shaken than me. There is a scene that still moves me in memory. Virtually a scene of tears. We were walking in Via Pietro Micca. Gianpiero wouldn't stop repeating, "How you've exposed yourself!" He was so emotional, so full of anger and regret, that there must have been all kinds of factors involved. His rapport with his family, certainly. His parents knew me well, esteemed me, often invited me to lunch. Years later it was I who was at the bedside of his dying mother. But at that moment it was his father who was ill with cancer. He was in anguish and vented his feelings to his oncologist: "I'm worried about my son. He lives with this gentleman older than he is."

At the same period I had almost wrapped up the negotiation for the apartment in Via Mazzini. But after this piece of publicity the landlord rang me up and said, "Professor, is what I read in the papers true?" "Yes it is." "Then you can forget about the apartment." Me: "If you like, we could talk it over."

So this old gentleman, who had lived in Africa for many years, received me. We talked, and he not only gave me the apartment, but he also voted for me.

In 1972 a Swedish professor from the University of Uppsala, whom I had met at an international conference, suggested that I replace him for a semester (it means four months there) in America. He requested it as a favor, but I jumped for joy. Imagine, teaching in the United States! Salary: $12,000 for the semester.

I already knew the language well, I read English, but to use it for teaching . . . I took an intensive course in English, expensive too, with the tapes, the headphones, everything. And off I went. Or rather off we went, because Gianpiero came with me. We used the cheapest airline, the Icelandic one. First we had to go to Luxembourg, spend a night there, and then take off for New York.

As soon as we arrived I rented a Volkswagen and got my first credit card, because in America they won't give you anything without a credit card.

I taught at the State University of New York in Albany, the state capital. SUNY has many campuses, and later, for example, I taught at Stony Brook on Long Island.

I gave two courses: one for freshmen, twice a week for an hour and a half, and a three-hour seminar once a week. At the start I talked a lot, blah blah blah, but only for fear of not understanding what the students might say to me. Actually, things went well.

The campus was a large quadrangle with four towers at the corners, and naturally you would get disoriented because everything was uniform.

To tell the truth, Albany could make you kill yourself. It was a small provincial city where I had an enormous apartment on the ground floor of a detached house, and a car. But when Gianpiero went back to Italy, I felt sad and very much alone.

I had more or less discovered a gay bar, but it was neither convenient nor near, and I wasn't yet brave enough to visit the saunas in New York City.

It really was a question of courage, not morality. I had come a long way from the Gianni Vattimo who had once become indignant with his own master, Pareyson, one evening in Trier. Whenever we went to conferences abroad, the Italian vice consul would always greet us, and would always inform the master and me about the local nightspots and prostitutes. "And if you want to have some fun. . . ." And I would get a bit annoyed. One evening we came across a lady who was offering herself brazenly, and I made a fuss about it with Pareyson: "It's shameful, prostitution is a dirty business." I was still very puritan. And he, to my great surprise, considering his sense of evil and sin, said to me, "Well, you know, come on, think of someone on a trip, someone alone, what is he supposed to do in the evening? If this service is available, it's better than ruining a family." At Albany I was away and alone, and at home in Turin I had my new family. But I was ready for the gay bars and the saunas.

I went to New York very often in any case. But it was to visit Paola and Ugo, a husband and wife who were friends of mine, affectionate and amusing. That's how I survived.

And I studied, naturally. In summer, before leaving, I had practically finished the book on Nietzsche that came out in 1974 with the title *Il soggetto e la maschera*. In America I worked on the notes, went to the library, had books within easy reach that I wouldn't have found in Italy.

Then I was invited back to Albany again for the autumn semester of 1973, and naturally I went.

Again Gianpiero accompanied me for a little while.

The thing I remember with most pleasure is the demonstration against Nixon, who began his second term in January 1973.

Gianpiero and I went to this huge demonstration in Washington; we took a bus full of left-wing types, the smoke from joints literally billowing in the air.

On the bus I met a boy who was translating Derrida, simpatico, attractive even, but Gianpiero was there with me. I was reading *Maurice,* E. M. Forster's posthumous book, in English.

That's how my international activity began. There had been a few precedents, important ones even, but this was my real beginning as an itinerant, globetrotting philosopher.

Sergio Mamino came from Mondovì. He was passionate about art, and to study art at that time you had to enroll in the faculty of letters and philosophy. He had discovered that his president was openly gay, and he wanted to meet me. He had also discovered that I lived up on the hill and had sent me a postcard at Valsalice from a vacation spot. I couldn't figure out who this Sergio was who was writing me.

Then in Turin he showed up in person. Meanwhile Gianpiero and I had moved to the attic in Via Mazzini. Sergio lived nearby. And at a certain point he said, "I want to move in with you two."

I immediately said no, in the name of monogamy, I suppose. So-called casual encounters were one thing, Sergio's request another. Naturally, Gianpiero was a little put out, too; he couldn't figure out what was going on.

But my instinctive refusal gradually yielded to the idea, which gradually grew stronger and more fascinating, of a species of commune, maybe a bit complicated from the sentimental point of view, but a realization of the '68 communal dream.

And then, I was traveling a lot. I was glad to leave these two boys together (Sergio was twenty years younger than I was). Better for them not to be alone, I thought, so they don't wind up running risks or getting themselves into trouble.

And with the certainty that they were fond of me, and I was fond of them.

33 | DEATH THREATS

It was the period when the Brigate Rosse, the Red Brigades, were killing people at the rate of one per day. Someone would wake up in the morning and . . . bang. The mayor, Diego Novelli, and the president of the Piedmont region, Aldo Viglione, were doing nothing but attending funerals.

It was at Turin that the first trial of the BR was going to be "celebrated," to use the curious Italian idiom: the historic nucleus of the BR, Curcio and Franceschini.

On November 16, 1977, they killed Carlo Casalegno.

On March 8, 1978, the trial started.

I was still president of the faculty of letters and philosophy.

On March 9, day two of the trial, I was presiding at a faculty council. At a certain point the secretary, Signora Gianonne, came in and said, "Professor, the Red Brigades have telephoned. They say they want to kill you."

Naturally, it shakes you up. I left the council immediately ("Sorry, have to go"), went to the president's office, and the first thing I did was phone home. They had called there too, and uttered the same threat. Gianpiero, like me, was half-dead with fright.

We were really concerned. I was known as a left-wing faculty president, and some of my friends who knew people who knew the Brigatisti told me, "Look, this is no joke. They have a list of those on the left who aren't with them, and they plan to blow them away. Norberto Bobbio heads it, but you're on it too." Oh, okay.

The police told me, "We'll put men outside your apartment, but you won't notice anything." Sure, how would I? The first thing the concierge said to me was "Look, there's a car parked outside with four heavies inside . . . they're either *caramba* (Carabinieri) or Brigatisti."

In any case, we moved in the same day with Angela and Mario, in Via Vespucci. And immediately word arrives—from friends of friends again—that they plan to burn our apartment that night. Gianpiero, defying danger, went back home to get the cat. He said, "Never shall the Siamese puss be the only one to suffer in all this."

At just this time Gianpiero had been invited to a festival of visual poetry at Verona. After spending a night at Angela's, Gianpiero, Sergio, and I left for Verona. We stayed at a small hotel; we moved around with great circumspection, and the day after, we left for Tuscany. We took refuge with the rich sister of a Turinese friend of mine (Anna Cataldi, who was then married to Giorgio Falck), who had a beautiful country place at Bolgheri.

We got there and shut ourselves in. When supplies ran out, we were forced to go out and do a bit of shopping, but always with great caution.

After a week we were starting to say, "Well, we can't stay here forever, let's go back to Turin."

We got everything organized, got the car ready, and just as we were about to leave, the radio informed us that Aldo Moro had been kidnapped. It was March 16, 1978.

We barricaded ourselves in the house once more. There were helicopters flying overhead all day. I said, "In a Diane with a Turin license plate, I don't know what might happen." At the time the Diane was a typically left-wing car, highly suspect.

We stayed a few more days, I don't remember how many, then for good or ill we had to go back to Turin.

But I began getting around exclusively by taxi. From the apartment to the university. From the university to the apartment.

Above all, being the real target, I went to live for a while in the apartment of the mother of Marziano Guglielminetti, in Corso Duca degli Abruzzi. She was at the seaside, and the place was empty.

One afternoon a colonel of the Carabinieri whom I knew because he wanted to get his university degree (he was later put in charge of the mounted Carabinieri as punishment for having been found in the P2 files), came to speak with me. He had been in command of the platoon of Carabinieri that guarded the trial of the Brigatisti, but at this point the trial was finished. Who knows what's on his mind, I thought. But it turned out he wanted me to let him off some examinations. And he was asking me to supervise his thesis. I dug in my heels a bit, and told him, "Go ask Nicola Tranfaglia" (if Nicola found out he'd throw a punch at me, and he might not be entirely wrong). The colonel shot back, "But Tranfaglia is one of our suspects." And indeed they had just searched Nicola's place because he was rumored to have known the supposed mastermind of the BR, Gianbattista Lazagna. "Better not, certainly, in that case," I said.

We started arguing, and our voices rose. Me: "You cops threw Giuseppe Pinelli out the window." Him: "You people wrecked the secret services." "But Pinelli. . . ." "But the secret services. . . ." Until the doorbell rang. I wasn't expecting anyone, and the place must have looked empty. Who could it be? The colonel whispered to me to hide and went to open the door holding a revolver about a meter long. It was only a missionary looking for donations.

But that was the time of fear.

34 REVOLUTIONARY MORALISM

One of my students went to jail for terrorism, too, found on some list, I believe. I don't think he'd pulled a trigger yet, but he was certainly one of the many who were semiclandestine, one of those pretending to be a worker: he would leave the house at 6:00 AM with his lunch pail, to make people think he was headed to the factory, but he didn't go there; I don't know exactly where he went.

He was drop-dead beautiful. But he had such revolutionary moralism. . . . He wrote letters from jail as though he were under a death sentence for being in the Resistance. Those in the Resistance actually did die, they were allowed some rhetoric, but him . . .

I said to myself: Is this supposed to be my new Nietzschean overman?

I was preparing a second edition of my book on Nietzsche. I wrote a new preface in which I stated that I had come to realize that the liberated man, Nietzsche's overman, could not be the professional revolutionary subject. Take power? Look how that turns out. You wind up in charge of the troops in Afghanistan . . . give me a break!

This was also the period of Autonomia. I was fond of the word "autonomy." Pity, then, that the *autonomi* sometimes did dreadful things. But the word itself already spoke a different notion of politics, the one I hold now: we should just obstruct the development of the system; it's the only thing we can do.

And it contained a hint of the idea of weakening as a way of eluding power. All powers, and at all levels.

Autonomia appeared to me a nonviolent form of anarchism. I didn't want to do violent things, but I was so fed up with the system of police repression and emergency powers that I didn't know what to say any more.

35 | WEAK THOUGHT

Weak thought got its name, *pensiero debole,* only in autumn 1979, and it became the title of a collection of essays—it seems incredible now, when everyone is shunning it like the plague—edited by Pier Aldo Rovatti and me in 1983.

In autumn 1979, more than fifteen years after my first "debilist" reading of Heidegger, the idea of the history of Being as that of its growing lighter and more distant assumed a firm contour in my mind. And as time went on, so did all that it entailed, and was still to yield in the years ahead.

I was increasingly excited by the idea of interpreting Heidegger from the viewpoint of weakening, rather than that of the wait for a new apparition of Being. And a host of other things went into it: my preference for a nonaggressive ethics, ecology. Even Arthur Schopenhauer became, along with Heidegger and Nietzsche, one of the components of this "interpretation." And my personal rereading of Christianity and religion was also taking shape.

In a little art gallery in Salerno I gave a paper entitled "Dialettica, differenza, pensiero debole" (Dialectic, difference, weak thought), which became the first essay in the edited collection of 1983.

What did Pier Aldo and I write in the introduction? For example, "Italian discourse on the crisis of reason still has too much nostalgia for metaphysics. And it fails to assume the full brunt of the experience of the forgetting of Being, or of the 'death of God,' which Heidegger and Nietzsche have announced to our culture." We backed all this up, and we expressed our hope for "a thought capable of articulating itself in the half-light" (one of my interpretations of Heidegger), a path forward that doesn't try to "rediscover the originary, true Being that metaphysics has forgotten, in its scientistic, technological success," but rather "a way to encounter Being once more as trace, recall, a Being used up and weakened, and on that account alone, worthy of attention," *an ethic of weakness* that we knew to be "not simple, much more costly, less reassuring." And again: "a difficult balance between contemplating the abyss of negativity and the cancellation of every origin." He and I were aware that we were speaking about a "metaphor, and in a certain way a paradox." But the conclusion was upbeat because "the price paid by potent reason strikingly limits the objects than can be seen and of which it is possible to speak." Amen.

Technology is relieving social relations of their weight, making them lighter, less heavy. The idea behind weak thought was to turn that to advantage, to the point of realizing a form of liberation. Emancipation through inflation: if you receive just one television channel, whatever it tells you seems like gospel truth; if you have twenty, you take it or leave it. And postmodernity, the end of rationalized society, that is, of society with central rationality—this is a serious development, an advance, in the crisis of reason.

A few years later, in 1989, when I published *La società trasparente* (The transparent society), I realized that once again I was using an oxymoronic title. Because in reality, it's anything but transparent: a society that has all the means for becoming transparent becomes in reality more confusional. But it's precisely in confusion that you're obliged to become an autonomous subject. It's what Nietzsche is saying when he writes that in accomplished nihilism, one either becomes an overman or one is lost. Paradoxically, it's in mass society that it becomes necessary to be an overman, because you have to become an autonomous interpreter. If you are hearing too many voices without inventing one of your own amid the rest, well, you're lost, you are no more, you disappear.

So weak thought was a strong theory, a strong philosophical proposal. And—it seemed to us—very civil too, very "reasonable," very "dialogic," very unarrogant, especially given that a predilection for a nonaggressive ethics did and does form part of weak thought.

Instead there was an uproar.

Years later, in a set of lectures delivered at Bologna at the invitation of Umberto Eco that became my book *Oltre l'interpretazione* (*Beyond Interpretation: The Meaning of Hermeneutics for Philosophy,* a book I dedicated to the memory of Gianpiero in 1994), I tried again to "dissipate various misunderstandings that have accumulated over the years regarding the significance of that theoretical proposal, primarily because the notion of weakness has been deliberately taken in too narrow and literal a sense." Wasted effort. The outcry is directed at me; Pier Aldo is less exposed, he doesn't get around, rarely writes in the newspapers. And it comes from little provincial Italy, absolutely not from the rest of the world. I am attacked on every possible front: personal, philosophical, political. Everyone piles on. And it shows no sign of waning.

Why?

The main reason lies, I believe, in the beginning. And when I say "beginning" I mean it seriously, not as a figure of speech.

My father Raffaele was born in 1885. He was a Calabrese peasant who emigrated to the north. He arrived in Turin in about 1910.

He was a policeman. One lasting memory I have—I don't know how, it must have been a phrase I heard in the house later—is that some evenings Papa "*era di cinta*" ("had perimeter duty"). I heard it as "*incinta*" (pregnant) and didn't understand it at all. It meant he was on duty outside the jail. I practically never knew him. I didn't have time; he died of pulmonitis (like my sister later) when I was barely sixteen months old.

My mother, Rosa, was fifteen years younger than him and came from Pinerolo. She was a seamstress.

My sister Liliana was an office employee.

My aunt Angiolina was a factory worker.

I was born at home, at 10 Via Germanasca, in Borgo San Paolo. Working-class homes. The homes of people who worked hard from morning to evening. Who had a hard time just keeping going. And they called me Gianteresio to keep both grandparents happy: grandpa Giovanni and grandma Teresa.

I was always out in the street, and I liked being there. I knew a ton of people. My earliest memories are of a coal and charcoal merchant, Signor Viarisio, with whom I spent a lot of time. Because he had his store out in the open, with containers that I turned into boats.

And then, a man who was always alone, on the ground floor of the house where we lived.

And my uncle's tobacco shop.

I remember the streets as the streets were then. I remember that before I was five, when I started going to school, I used to go with my mother to do the shopping.

Those are my origins. Roots in the south. An immigrant father. Dignified poverty. I, a child half-orphaned.

If I let the memories flow, I realize that some happy and important moments in my life have had to do with terraces: the terrace at Cetraro, the terrace of the house in Heidelberg, the terrace at Santorini. Even here in Via Po, where I live now, there's a small terrace full of plants.

But there is another terrace that has caused, and still causes me, a bit of hurt as well as anger, a metaphorical yet very concrete terrace, the "Roman terrace," which is a familiar Italian codeword for a certain blend of social, cultural, and intellectual snobbery.

I believe that is the main reason for the violence of the attacks on me and on weak thought, or on weak thought and me, which comes to the same thing. There are others, but that's the principal reason. My international standing, the conferences, the books translated into dozens of languages, even my outing, my media presentability (certainly not any striving for media presence), the "prestigious" friendships that I have gained over time and with my work, have all opened a bit of a breach, no doubt. But the "Roman terrace" is always there and it keeps on trying. Doesn't give up, doesn't let go.

Who in Italy cares about philosophical speculation? To whom do you think it matters—unfortunately—if thought is weak or strong?

And yet it took Carlo Sini about one minute to start saying that weak thought was rubbish. As for Massimo Cacciari—let's not even go there.

A day doesn't pass without somebody taking a swipe at it in public. Maybe they don't see the paradox, but what they've achieved is to make me the only Italian philosopher well known to the public, and well known for his own original elaboration, for his thought, not because he's the mayor of someplace or a participant in a reality show.

In 1985 Gianpiero and I always used to watch Renzo Arbore's *Quelli della notte,* one of the most successful shows on Italian television. And every evening Roberto D'Agostino would repeat this tagline: "*pensiero debole, debolismo reaganiano*" (weak thought, Reaganite debilism). Gianpiero and I laughed, naturally. But I still don't know how dozens of my colleagues kept from bursting with envy. Maybe they never knew. Distinguished philosophers don't watch Renzo Arbore.

And I'd like someone to show me an analogy, from the last hundred years, to what happened with weak thought. How many people go to a book presentation, a debate about a philosophical concept (excluding the festivals, which are trendy and recent)? Twenty people. Fifty when it's a deluxe affair. But in the middle of the 1980s the debates on weak thought were jammed with people. You could have charged admission. True, it was full of people who were protesting: "It's shameful, it isn't true that thought is weak, neocapitalism, blah blah blah." But they came. They got worked up. The "enemy" was never them.

When I was running for the European Parliament, Francesco Merlo saw fit to deride me mercilessly in the pages of *Corriere della Sera.*

Recently someone mentioned Carlo Ginzburg to me. Because when he did an interview with *La Repubblica,* the first question (without naming me explicitly) just happened to be about weak thought. Ginzburg, looking down his nose: "Oh . . . yes . . . weak thought," as though it were obvious that it was an idiocy that wasn't even worth dwelling on. Ginzburg wears a majestic air, and he does some interesting research certainly, perhaps a bit otiose, but that's his business, I don't have any objection. But when I publicly urged Adriano Sofri not to accept a pardon from Berlusconi—you've held out this long, stand firm a little longer, I told him—well, Ginzburg rushed indignantly to call my position shameful.

And Toni Negri, in his little book *La differenza italiana,* calls me a poor chap who is just passing by.

In 1977 I went to the famous conference against repression at Bologna. I went with a pair of extremist friends and a few other scruffy types in my red Volkswagen, and the police searched us down to our underwear. I waved to Gilles Deleuze from a distance, and nearby was Giulio Einaudi. Such an elegant revolutionary, with his leather jacket.

Some hostilities are intellectual, arising out of different schools and styles of thought, and they don't necessarily turn personal. I've had those with Emanuele Severino, Mario Perniola, Valerio Verra, Carlo Sini, Vittorio Mathieu, Massimo Cacciari, too, when it comes right down to it. And naturally that hard-bitten Thomist, Umberto Eco. And those are one thing.

But someone like Marcello Pera, who when he wrote for *La Stampa* (the same paper I wrote for) never missed a chance to fling mud at the "weak thinker"—that's different. I was about to quit the paper, but luckily he left first.

Carlo Augusto Viano had invented the expression "weak reason" before me, which I practically copied with my "weak thought."

When my definition came out, he dashed off a booklet against me—which soon sank from public notice—entitled *Va pensiero* (Go, thought). I shot back with an article called "Ma va là pensiero" (Ah, go on, thought) because it was an intolerable thing. This hostility, though, has faded away with the passage of time, to the point of vanishing.

The best I can hope for is a sort of friendly paternalism, such as I get from Aldo Cazzullo. He included me among Italy's thirty-three "senior statesmen" along with Umberto Veronesi, Alberto Arbasino, Gino Paoli, Fernanda Pivano, Pietro Ingrao, Mario Monicelli, and so on, but he wrote, "Vattimo's extraordinary intelligence ought to be protected against itself. He should be compelled to say no to a few of his countless interviewers. But the reprobate always answers." Right. The next time I'll say no to you, Cazzullo my friend. Look at the old driveller blathering away about Iraq and the Turin Olympics, Thales the philosopher and Paolo Bonolis the television host, writes Cazzullo, implying that for me there's no difference.

One day I asked Cesare Cases: "Sorry, but why did you at Einaudi publish that fool Verrecchia while I had to go to all the way to Milan to publish my Nietzsche book with Bompiani?" Cases: "We decided that we needed an anti-Vattimo at our publishing house." Ah. So there we have it. I didn't fit in. I didn't have the right credentials. And I didn't have the necessary family background. Anacleto Verrecchia is one of those people who call Nietzsche a dolt because, unlike Schopenhauer, he didn't frequent bordellos and wasn't a suave socialite. Verrecchia wrote a biography of Nietzsche entirely built up around episodes such as Nietzsche losing his luggage, Nietzsche forgetting his umbrella, and so on. Verrecchia was a retailer of anecdotes, not a philosopher, but he published with Einaudi.

And where do you think I met Mario Mieli? At a march in front of Fiat? At a gay pride demonstration? No, not exactly. I met him at the home of Marco Vallora's parents, highly respectable folk, musicians, people who knew the *crème de la crème*. And Mario Mieli was there with Giulio Einaudi. Of course Mieli could publish his *Elementi di critica omosessuale* (Elements of homosexual critique) with Einaudi: he was a cousin of Paolo Mieli.... For heaven's sake, I don't have anything against the Mieli family, but the point is that there are no other genuine reasons. It's not even that I'm a fag. It's a simple, unalloyed, straightforward question of social class.

There's a sort of *conventio ad excludendum* on the part of those who come from the Communist Party, and even more on the part of those who left it at some point, like Giuliano Ferrara. I am convinced that Massimo D'Alema is a better friend to Giuliano Ferrara than to me, even though I was elected to the European Parliament for five years on the Democratic Party of the Left slate: D'Alema's party, the Left Democrats, not Berlusconi's. Ah, the unbearable susceptibility of the left, these personalities who, the more they quit walking the walk, the louder they talk the progressive talk, acting like they own it.

I admit it: they succeed in always making me feel a bit out of place. There's nothing I can do. I feel like a parvenu, and I always will. Class tells, you could say, reversing the usual meaning.

I've always said that I'm someone who could go to dinner with the "Avvocato" (the late Gianni Agnelli), but couldn't bring anyone with me.... Because I don't have relatives, I'm not on the inside, and there is always this mental reserve, this web of impatience with respect to me. It's class-based reserve; I'm a proletarian, it can't be helped. An intellectual I may be, but first and foremost I come from the lower depths, I'm not well-born, I've come from nowhere, and as if that weren't enough—I'm a miserable ex-Catholic.

My father was Calabrese. And he was a policeman.

38 | A SAFE PAIR OF HANDS

When it comes to personalities I don't esteem, I get irritated, but in the end I lose interest. Early on Pareyson warned me about another aspect of power: "As long as you don't occupy a real place in the world, everyone's your friend; when you do start gaining a place, watch out." Indeed. Indeed I can't even get one of my students an academic job anymore. Because you need alliances, and I'm a "maestro without portfolio."

But with the others, with the real "greats," with persons for whom I feel admiration and gratitude, I've discovered that inside I bear a *conventio ad excludendum* against myself, a doubt that rationally I know I oughtn't to have. But that I do have. Does it come from my class roots, too? From some psychological insecurity? From both? I don't know. I do know for sure that when Gadamer wrote me letters full of respect and consideration, when Rorty stated that I had understood things and praised me for a difficult job well done, I was surprised to find myself asking: Who knows if they're saying that because they mean it, or from courtesy? Almost a feeling that I'm secretly putting one over on them, as though it were all a bluff. I know it's not, and yet this insecurity periodically surfaces.

It could also be read as a form of "weak happiness," as an offshoot of my stupor at having got where I am, and where I certainly never dreamed I would get.

With people in general it's like that. On one hand, faced with an attack full of gratuitous hatred, I think, with childish surprise: How can they not be fond of someone like me? On the other, I always think that I'm incapable of winning over anyone, of deserving anyone's affection. If someone does show me affection, simply and naturally and without expecting anything in return, I almost wonder how it's possible. But it's because I'm the sort who, for example during the work on the *Enciclopedia filosofica,* was able to calm down even Livio Garzanti when he flew into a rage. Paolo De Benedetti, who worked at Garzanti, always used to say, "You're a safe pair of hands."

I know my own fragilities and insecurities all too well.

Weak thought was officially born in autumn 1979, and that same winter I met Richard Rorty, a philosopher and a friend who became increasingly important for me.

I was invited to a meeting on the postmodern at the University of Wisconsin at Milwaukee (that's right, Jeffrey Dahmer's town).

Richard Rorty heard me speak and told me, "I'd like a copy of your paper." I was flattered. But better yet, he gave me a copy of his book *Philosophy and the Mirror of Nature*.

I went back to Italy, finished my lectures at the university, left for Santorini on vacation, and read *Philosophy and the Mirror of Nature*. I used to read in the morning before the sun got too high, and in the evening once the sun went down. Again on a splendid terrace. Again a fulguration, enormous enthusiasm. I discovered we were each saying more or less the same thing.

Rorty is one who maintains—and this is what made such an impression on me—that the greatest philosophers of the twentieth century were John Dewey, Ludwig Wittgenstein, and Martin Heidegger. Nobody had ever put them together before. It was a revolutionary idea, enticing.

That was an important moment because I began to feel myself to be more than just some little Italian linked only to the Italian situation, someone—how to put it?—who cast a shadow internationally. If there was also someone in the United States saying the same things . . .

And from that was born a new effort to understand the post-analytics, those thinkers who emerged after analytic philosophy, and who still interest me a lot: Rorty *in primis*. But not just him.

If you think about what goes on in Italy, about the fact that it's dangerous just to be mistaken for a "weak thinker," you can imagine what it meant for me that Rorty—whose correct label is "neopragmatist"—chose to call himself a "weak thinker" at a conference in London.

To crisscross Italy, to travel round the world, to meet thousands of persons of every sort and in every continent, to give lectures, conference papers, debates—all this has been one of the nicest, luckiest parts of my life, and still is. It comprises an almost infinite spectrum of sensations: fatigue, amusement, gratification, affection, emotion, worry, novelty, intellectual stimulus.

One of my first conference papers outside Italy, maybe the first period, was at the Sorbonne in Paris, no less, where I met Mikel Dufrenne.

Then, in July 1964, I wasn't even thirty, Gilles Deleuze invited me to the international conference on Nietzsche at Royaumont, and there—as well as getting to know Michel Foucault, Pierre Klossowski, Henri Birault—I saw Karl Löwith, whom I already knew from Heidelberg, again. I also met Gabriel Marcel, whom I noticed crying with emotion during my talk. Oh God, I thought. Later they told me he always cried, he was elderly and couldn't control his tears, and that put the matter a bit more into perspective.

There were the meetings of the International Aesthetics Committee, at one of which, still very young and quite involuntarily, of course, but through one of those pieces of carelessness that I regard as among the worst sins of my life, I revealed the political secret of a Romanian philosopher, a secret that was meant to stay secret.

There were choices that were, let's say, extravagant. When you're a young intellectual, the last thing you do is burden yourself with particular worries and scruples; today I would, of course. The first time I went to Spain as a philosopher, it was with Opus Dei. And in 1978, out of a lust for travel that Dufrenne and I shared, and also a bit out of playfulness, an urge to go and say revolutionary things even in an ultrareactionary milieu, I went with him, at his urging, to give a lecture in the United States at the Reverend Moon's cultural institute. Knowing full well that nobody ever pays close attention anyway, which they didn't.

Every encounter leaves some kind of mark on you. When I was invited to a major conference on Italian thought held at New York University, I met Francesco Pellizzi, the son of Camillo, the first Italian professor of sociology. Francesco, one of the owners of the publishing house Adelphi, a great friend of Roberto Calasso, put me up at his place, casually the first time and without knowing me, but then we became friends, and it often happened that he would go away for the weekend and leave the apartment to me, where I slept in a room with an Andy Warhol hanging on the wall. The building was on East 74th Street, near the Metropolitan Museum and close to where Woody Allen then lived.

This year I gave the opening address at the International Hegel Congress at Poznan, in Poland, and the Mediterranean Congress on Aesthetics at Portorose in Slovenia.

In Italy there were the so-called Perugia meetings for a few years, organized by American philosophers, to which we Italians were invited as well: Cacciari, Perniola, Severino, Verra, Vitiello, Sini, Vattimo. Sometimes Gadamer.

There was the Institute of Philosophical Studies of Enrico Castelli (full name: Enrico Castelli-Gattinara di Zubiena, if you take my meaning), who had money to spend, thanks to his Christian Democratic connections, but who at least organized a high-level, and very productive, international colloquy every year. Paul Ricoeur, Gadamer, Levinas, American philosophers, all came. I met a few of the theologians of the death of God there: Thomas Altizer and Gabriel Vahanian. I'm still in contact with Vahanian. Altizer I saw again at Stony Brook when I taught there for a spell.

In 1974 my book on Nietzsche came out, and in 1975 the left won the local and regional elections, so along with my university job, I began making the rounds of the local culture departments. Debates all the time. What I call "the Nietzsche circle" was formed, because we were always on the same bill: Cacciari, Bodei, Masini, Rella, Rovati, Vattimo. Naturally, mine wasn't the only book that came out; the others published as well.

A few of these colleagues had become known through a collection edited by Aldo Giorgio Gargani of the University of Pisa, *La crisi della ragione* (The crisis of reason). As a Heideggerian, I wasn't asked to contribute, but they did invite me to the debates.

And there was a really interesting period when I was sought out by specialists from other "territories" who thought I might have something to say from the philosophical point of view. Architects and psychoanalysts, essentially. I took these gatherings seriously, but it seemed to me I had more to learn than to teach. I was drifting close to postmodernism, and the architects took an interest when, in considering Paolo Portoghesi's *Via Novissima* at the Venice Biennale, I dwelt on the free utilization of historical forms. For the architects—meaning Philip Johnson and Bob Venturi—this meant utilizing forms outside their context, or reviving anachronistic ones, freeing oneself from the cages of formal respect for history:

pick and choose freely, history doesn't constrain us anymore, it's a repertory of forms we can freely utilize.

This was a postmodern attitude, in my view. I always cite Nietzsche's image of modern man wandering around in history as if it were a theme park or a storehouse of theatrical masks. Putting them on, taking them off. Nietzsche meant it as denigration, but at the end of his life, when he was already crazy—but how crazy was he, really?—he wrote, and this is incredible: "I am all the names of history, I am the Pharaoh Cambyses, I am Alois Negrelli (the planner of the Suez canal), I am Alessandro Antonelli (who built the Mole Antonelliana in Turin)." That is, he discovers that his own youthful objection against historicism, which was that "things are all mixed up today," is, on the contrary, the only salvation: to ransack history, without caring in the least about determined and determining belongings.

The other aspect of the postmodern is the impossibility of a totally rational construction. At a Michigan university, I've seen a campus built with a play of so many perspectives that your gaze can't take it in all at once.

Psychoanalysts, especially the Milan group around Diego Napolitani, warm to another of my crucial themes: interpretation, in place of the nude, crude, putatively objective, fact. They essentially work with interpretation too. Napolitani has read Gadamer, my introduction to *Verità e metodo* (*Truth and Method*). It was actually from Gadamer that I learned how every experience of truth is an interpretative experience, a theme developed further by my master, Pareyson, than by Gadamer himself. An act of knowing is an affair that concerns both you and the object you are interpreting: the person of the other, the work you are reading. You yourself change as you interpret that thing, but the thing changes too, because a new interpretation is stuck onto it. This approach has led me to a vision of history that I've held to ever since, not just of human finiteness to be accepted positively, but also of a certain randomness in history, which should also be lived positively: there are authors whom I will never understand, or understand only vaguely, and that is not terrible but beautiful. There are works that pass into history and others that don't, but that doesn't mean that objectively the former were better than the others that vanished.

I've always thought that philosophy should be useful and closely interwoven with life. With these types who aren't philosophers I always feel a bit ill at ease, fearful I won't have anything to say. I know I've learned. From the psychoanalysts, for example, the art of staying quiet, waiting a bit, saying things that may not pertain directly, because that's what they do. Ill at ease as well because I, a philosopher, have a systematic mind: I always have to know where we are starting from, where we'll wind up, the how and the why. They have encouraged me to go ahead and try things out, discuss, experiment.

Yet the event that moves me most in memory was a major Catholic conference at Rome, to which Pareyson, naturally, brought me along. In coming to terms with my Catholicism and my Maoism, I had begun to think that Karl Barth's "totally other" God was perhaps really the "future God" of Ernst Bloch. Even just to refer to Bloch was revolutionary and scandalous for official Catholics.

So in 1969 this big meeting of the association of Catholic university instructors, headed by Gabrio Lombardi, Augusto Del Noce, and Vittorio Mathieu, was held at Rome. My whole paper focused on liberation theology. Blazing scandal. The only reason they didn't hurl rotten tomatoes at me was because the protocols of this solemn gathering didn't allow for it.

We were in a small theater in Borgo Pio. Only one person defended me (apart from Pareyson, who sat there shivering quietly).

He was named Santino Caramella, and later I came across him in some history of Sicilians on the left . . .

Del Noce and Mathieu kept insisting that what I had said was inconceivable. Gabrio Lombardi didn't even say a word.

But it was great, above all because I went to Rome by car with my new companion, Gianpiero, whom I'd known since the previous autumn. We had a lot of fun.

By 1969 I no longer cared. I was shortly to make full professor, but I had already been a tenured assistant professor for a year, which gave me self-confidence and serenity. It meant they couldn't get rid of me unless they caught me trying to burn the university down. They couldn't take away my job. I had Gianpiero. I was happy.

We stayed in a pensione in Piazza Campo Marzio, an ex-bordello to which a Roman friend had directed me because there I could come and go as I wished, with whom I wished, when I wished. The Nuovo Olimpia movie house was close by, and so was the lower house of the Italian Parliament. If the film had suddenly broken and the lights had come on, there would have been a whole lot of trousers and underwear being pulled up.

41 | IN HISTORY

Heidegger thinks that Being is not structure but occurrence, that which eventuates in history in different cultures, in different epochs. He puts a lot of emphasis on the notion of epoch. Epoch is historical epoch, but also—from the Greek—suspension. A historical epoch is a freezing of the constellations, an interval in the movement of the heavens. In the epochs, different horizons open up, with different truth criteria. Sometimes it's believed that there are vampires, other times that there are atoms.

How are historical epochs inaugurated, according to Heidegger? For him the opening, inaugurating events are the great works of art. It is the great work of art that founds an epoch of Being, an illumination that makes the truth "eventuate."

However, in an essay written long ago, he states that the modes of truth's eventuation may also be diverse. He alludes to them a bit mysteriously, but speaks of the foundation of a new state. Or the essential sacrifice, the supreme ethical act. . . . But after that he never speaks about these things again.

If Heidegger always remained rather reactionary, the reason lies—I'm inclined to say, provocatively—even deeper than his involvement with Nazism. It's because he looks for the originary event of an epoch in the poets or in the words of the pre-Socratics. He always thought that in order to understand modernity one could read Hölderlin, the "poets in time of privation." What he actually believed was that the great work of art par excellence is the Bible; and the Bible is effectively the institution of the West, with its disputes over how many angels can dance on the head of a pin, its bloodshed over the interpretation of scripture. That's the great classic.

In 2003 they invited Jürgen Habermas and me (in that order, obviously) to give the two introductory speeches at the World Congress of Philosophy in Istanbul. And it was there that I stuck my neck out and said: Why not speak of political eventuation as well? The French Revolution was the opening of an epoch too. Obviously! So then, why shouldn't we to be able to say that truth eventuates—other than in some mysterious word that only a few people understand—in the election results?

Among the passages from Hölderlin cited most frequently by Heidegger, there's a particularly beautiful one: "Because mankind has named many gods since we have been a colloquy."

If Being eventuates in history, it eventuates in historical languages, and so in language, in the dialogue among humans, in the human conversation.

This word "conversation"—which I like a lot more than "dialogue"—has recently been foregrounded by Santiago Zabala. I find it a brilliant intuition, drawn a bit from Rorty, a bit from Gadamer, but a fascinating novelty. These openings occur in language, in the historical languages.

Here you can see the full meaning of the title of my book *Essere, storia e linguaggio in Heidegger,* which closely interweaves these three elements: Being, history, language.

Heidegger is one who no longer thinks of Kantian reason as something eternal, with a capital R, but as something historically given. Kant's a priori are given to us in the historical language that we speak. When we predicate being of something—the donkey is, or the donkey has four hooves—we are producing a theory of it, using time, space, and the categories.

When I predicate being of a thing—such and such a thing is—truth lies in the assertion, not in the single word. If I say "unicorn,"

I'm not saying anything. If I say, "The unicorn is or is not," I am saying something. This also means suspending the peremptoriness of that which we say "is."

For Kant, time, space, and the categories are equal in all men; therefore science (in his case, Newtonian science) has universal value. But not for Heidegger. Not by a long shot.

Nothing eludes historicity, least of all philosophy and thought. So it follows, not that Heidegger was more intelligent than Kant, but that he came 120 years after Kant. And in that stretch of time there arose cultural anthropology, psychology . . . sciences, ways of knowing that cause the idea that reason is always the same in all epochs and in all humans to crumble.

Heidegger takes this into account in putting the problem of what Being means, whether it is supposed to function even for us, who are finite entities that are born, die, have problems. The upshot is that Being, for Heidegger—well, to tell the truth, I don't exactly know what it is, and neither does he. He does know for sure that it cannot be an object. Ultimately it's this "thing" in quotation marks that announces itself in the languages of the cultures within which we are always already thrown.

Being therefore eventuates in language. But how? In conversation. In the living language, that is, that a humanity speaks. Naturally it—Being—isn't an offshoot of language, but that's its mode of occurrence.

And if Being is eventuation, we may further suppose that Being is nothing other than this: the meaning of the word "Being" in the history of our language, and in the use we make of it.

And indeed, where else would Being be, if not in the history of the word?

One of my great "finds"—the one that caused Gadamer to remark that I was a real philosopher—has been this idea that to rethink Being, as Heidegger does in *Being and Time,* is to shift the ground from under that which we take to be grounded, set it in relation to a history without end.

You're like an ape in a cage. The cage is the a priori of your epoch, but when you set it in relation to history, go back in history, move back and forth, what do you accomplish? It's not that you find a more stable cage to go to; all you are doing is shaking your cage.

And here is where Heidegger uses expressions such as "to leap into the abyss," "to leap into Being as abyss." But the abyss is really abyssal, in the sense that you never get to a more stable point, far from it.

Philosophy winds up being a sort of suspension of the peremptoriness of the things that eventuate, that are there. Plato thought of philosophy as that which grounded the other knowledges. I think of philosophy—I, not Heidegger—as that which shifts the ground from under knowledges. In the sense that it causes them to be seen as dependent on this historicity of Being that is, as it were, lost in origins that are never very clear, in myth. . . . Gianbattista Vico might have agreed with me.

From this perspective, not even science is an enemy any longer—I grasped this more clearly reading Gadamer—but it does have to be dominated politically. Philosophy must regulate relations, just as everyday language must govern specialized languages, and common political ethics must impose rules on the sciences.

Once again Santiago Zabala has summed it up well in his introduction to the "dialogue" between me and Rorty on the future of religion: "Wherever there is an authority that, in the guise of a scientific or ecclesiastical community, imposes something as objective truth, philosophy has the obligation to proceed in the opposite direction: to show that truth is never objectivity, but always interpersonal dialogue which takes effect in the sharing of a language."

Postmodernity is the milieu where what Heidegger predicted in his essay "The Age of the World Picture" is realized. It's an important essay for me.

In that essay he portrays the modern society of his epoch, the epoch of scientific specialization. Sciences grow more specialized, so we are always learning more and more, but gradually these specializations construct images of the world irreconcilable among themselves. So that in the end there's something like an explosion, an impossibility of having an image of the world. In my view (although Heidegger never said so), this is what the postmodern is: it's the idea of a society over which no single principle can exercise domination any longer.

The idea of the postmodern as fragmented society is found in Jean-François Lyotard. That was another important reading for me. Lyotard and I became friends, and he came to Turin to teach for some months.

Modernity is self-consuming, it consumes itself with the dissolution of strong rationality, the central rationalities, with this crisis of visions of the world no longer able to unify themselves. With the multiplicity of the sciences. But that's what's good about the postmodern.

How did we arrive at this? How did we arrive at ceasing to believe in history as something unitary and progressive, something that, as it moves along, is going forward toward completeness? When the colonial peoples compel us, in point of fact, no longer to be Eurocentric, because if there is a unitary line in history it's the one we Europeans have drawn. Nobody ever dreamed that the unitary line of history went through China. It went here. The others were primitives, barbarians, underdeveloped.

When—and we realized this above all at the time of the oil crisis, in the 1970s—we could no longer refer to the Arabs as poor devils, because if they turned off the taps we'd all be in big trouble, at that point the colonial era was really over.

From then on history is no longer thinkable as a linear and unitary process, and the full weight of the plurality of cultures and languages makes itself felt willy-nilly. We receive the words of other cultures, or rather, the other cultures start talking for themselves, and maybe firing rifles too, forcing us to think differently.

Once again, this idea is closely connected to my Heideggerism. Heidegger doesn't think that Being can be known in the way that Aristotle and Plato conceived it, that is, that there is a hard core, a *primum,* because Being thought in that way is only one more object among many.

Incapable of thinking Being in that way, Heidegger's philosophy responds to historico-destinal events. That is, not only did the Berlin wall come down, but in that moment the world changed.

This is the postmodern too: to correspond to Being means to correspond to its pluralization.

From that one also arrives at the idea that if someone wants to maintain central rationality with force, he is a dangerous enemy. And you can take up arms against him, for example.

A few classical Marxist thinkers reply that we postmodernists are cheerleaders for late capitalism.

The very idea. I couldn't care less if they call me that. But naturally, I think they have it all wrong.

There is a page in Heidegger that I have twisted and turned in every possible way, because it's the only one in which he says that maybe the new event of Being, an eventuation of Being different from metaphysics, can come about in the ensemble of the technological world, which may be the extreme point of damnation, the most total forgetting of Being, but might also turn out to be a first flash of the event.

Surprising. Gadamer personally confirmed to me that when Heidegger made that statement during a lecture, it wasn't just an offhand remark. Indeed, he was perfectly well aware of the "scandalous" character of what he was saying. Except that he never said it again.

In the same text, Heidegger maintains that this possible flashing of a new mode of Being's eventuation in the totality of the technological world cannot correspond to a return to the pre-Socratics. Rather, it comes about in the technological world, because there man and world lose the characters of subject and object that metaphysics had conferred upon them.

This leads me to think that Heidegger must have had in mind a possibility, however inchoate, of a new mode of Being no longer grounded in the subjectivization of the subject and the objectivization of the world. And that led me to think a lot about the information society, the electronic society, about problems that are current right now: the copyright of everything that goes onto the Internet . . . which is also a way to raise doubts about the whole structure of property: who gets paid for the copyright?

And I'm inclined to think that late modernity, as well as being a time of great peril, might be just the opposite, something exciting and different.

Young people have never read a book? Okay, maybe so, it's monstrous, but who knows how many other things they have discovered in the meantime?

So I think of what's happening the world right now not in purely negative terms, but also in providential ones. Where the danger grows, there also grows that which saves: another line of Hölderlin that Heidegger often cites.

45 | OBITUARIES

Gianpiero was only forty-three when he died, shortly after Christmas 1992.

Sergio died at forty-seven, just before Easter 2003.

Julio died not long after Gianpiero.

I practically never knew my father; he died when I was sixteen months old.

My mother died twenty years ago now, in 1980, at age eighty.

My sister Liliana died three years after our mother, in 1983; she was only fifty-three. An absurd death, a case of the flu that turned into pulmonitis and that nobody could diagnose or cure. The tragic fire in the Statuto movie theater happened just then, and when I was with her at the hospital, at one point I started to see all these injured people arriving.

I've outlived those dearest to me, outlived my family.

For the first time, I'm alone.

And I've become an expert in a very special literary genre, the obituary.

For Gianpiero I chose these words from the breviary: "*Salva nos, Domine, vigilantes, custodi nos dormientes*" (Save us, O Lord, while awake, guard us while we sleep).

For Sergio, on the other hand, a line from psalm 125: "*Magnificavit Dominus facere nobiscum*" (What marvels he did for us).

And that was how my friends ended.

There's a poem by a minor German poet of the nineteenth century, set to music by Mahler in *Kindertotenlieder,* that goes like this: "Be not sad, I have only gone out for a long walk." I put those lines at the beginning of the book I dedicated to Gianpiero. They still make me shiver.

I only cry when I reread the obituaries. The feeling of loss, once formulated, moves one even more profoundly.

46 | OBITUARIES TWO: CACCIARI

On the other hand, I wouldn't know how to write an obituary of Massimo Cacciari. Nor of Umberto Eco, come to that. It won't be necessary. I wish both of them a long life, and I hope to go before they do, even if I'm 120 years old. But I wouldn't know what to write. I've never really understood what the devil it is Cacciari is saying or thinking.

Once—many years ago—Cacciari sent an article to the *Rivista di estetica,* which I edited with Pareyson. Pareyson comes in and says to me, "Try reading this, will you, to see if you can understand anything, because I can't." I read it diligently and couldn't understand anything either. So I said to the master, "I understand nothing, but if you wish we can publish it anyway." Finally, though, we decided to reject it.

When I saw him, I said, "Massimo, I'm very fond of you, but I don't understand a word of what you write. Come on, enlighten me, speak up, explain." And his answer was, "Your fondness is obviously making you blind." That's still a gag line between us.

But gags apart, what kind of philosophical position does Cacciari hold? Who knows? He writes as though Hegel had died yesterday. He always takes up where the idealists left off, he goes around and around.

Here's a confession: when I wrote *Credere di credere* (To believe that one believes) in 1998, I wrote it against Cacciari. His name doesn't appear in the book, but he's the one who was always talking about angels while insisting he was not a believer. Then why the devil keep talking about angels? I don't get it. Clue me in, will you?

With Umberto Eco it's a whole other story.

Even though I couldn't write his obit, because I don't believe he has said anything new in philosophy. He has made advances in semiotics, but since I don't understand anything about semiotics, I'd still be unable to write a word.

Eco finished his degree with Pareyson before I did. He jumped through the same hoops I did. But our common master didn't back him for a full professorship. Indeed, when I won the competition for the chair in esthetics, Eco was a participant.

I tried to keep things cordial between Pareyson and Eco, but Pareyson kept complaining about him. He was very susceptible about personal things. Umberto had a bit of a sharp tongue, and on top of that he had become friends with Enzo Paci in Milan, writing for *aut aut*. And if there was one thing that terrorized Pareyson, it was the prospect of one of his students defecting to someone else. So all this got the master a bit twitchy. But he was certainly convinced that Eco was clever. I'm afraid he may even have thought he was smarter than me.

What did he complain about? That Eco didn't send him greetings at Christmas. That was what earned me the chair, I believe. And yet I used to say to Pareyson, "Look, Eco isn't like you and me, he is incapable of writing 'best wishes.' Either he finds an amusing way to say it or he doesn't say it at all." That's still my view. I can't imagine Eco taking a nice Christmas card with a manger or a Christmas tree and some curlicues and writing, "Dear professor, my best wishes to you." Whereas the rest of us did so, miserable provincials that we were. When I published a book, especially before I won my chair, I would send copies to a whole mailing list of professors: "To professor so-and-so, devoted homage from Gianni Vattimo." *Devoto omaggio*? I don't believe Umberto Eco ever wrote that to anyone in his life. Presumptuous as he is. Justifiably.

Umberto is the only person I don't envy for being more intelligent than I am. I've had a few polemics with him recently, but it was just needling, fodder for the newspapers, trifles. My affection, my friendship, my admiration for him are truly great.

In Italy we hardly see each other; neither of us has much time. Sometimes we meet in New York. There we both have more free time, so it's long walks and long debates and gossip in Piedmontese dialect, because Eco is from Alessandria and it matters to him. I get a real kick out of seeing people swivel around and whisper, "Who is that with Umberto Eco?"

I've always considered him an old friend; but he's also been a sort of older comrade or vice maestro to me.

He's taught me so many things. Mainly he taught me funny stories. I have a repertory of stories that would make Berlusconi jealous. Why? Because I've always hung out with Eco.

It would be better if he behaved a bit less like a monument, but nobody's perfect.

I'm convinced that when the next Italian wins the Nobel Prize in literature (once enough time has passed since Dario Fo's win), it will be a showdown between Claudio Magris, someone else who increasingly behaves like his own monument, and Umberto Eco. I'm betting on Eco; he has more arrows in his quiver. It'll certainly be a fine contest.

In saying that one of those two will win the Nobel Prize, I'm also saying that I'm already tickled at the thought of the loser grinding his teeth with rage.

They say there comes a critical age for everyone. For some it's their thirties, others their forties or their fifties. Not for me. To me that hasn't happened. For me it's been more like the seasons changing, from summer to winter, not an illumination but a darkening of the sky, an onset of overcast weather.

After the idyllic years, our family life began to grow unhappy. The rivalry between Gianpiero and Sergio increased; it was as if they were older and younger brothers. Sergio sulked a lot. Gianpiero got angry. Only on vacation all together were we still happy, like before, we three and Angela and Mario.

We changed apartments again. My friend Franco Debenedetti lived on the tenth and eleventh floors of the Torre Littoria, and he told me there was an apartment free. We celebrated the New Year there in 1983. And we lived in that apartment for five years, give or take.

There was a lot of competition to get into that building, but I succeeded. The reward was Sergio and Gianpiero squabbling over the furniture (I was paying for Sergio's analysis at that time) and remorseful self-torment for me. I had the impression of having become too rich, of no longer being what I once was. Via Mazzini was beautiful, but it was an attic, and now we were living in a real, luxurious apartment.

But things had been going that way for a while. In 1978 Gianpiero's father died at age sixty-three, and that was sad and difficult.

Then, to top things off, Gianpiero got AIDS. I think it was in a sauna at Nice in the autumn of 1985 while I was teaching in the United States for my usual semester.

Back in Turin in January 1986, and just turned fifty, I was recording a series of television programs for *La Clessidra* to be broadcast in the spring, a project they had asked me for and that I had written. It consisted of discussions between me and other philosophers, and it was the high point of my public success in Italy. And in due course they were broadcast; the first went out on April 19 at 7:30 on Raitre. I published all of them in the book *Filosofia al presente* (Philosophy at Present). The other philosophers were Francesco Barone, Remo Bodei, Italo Mancini, Vittorio Mathieu, Mario Perniola, Pier Aldo Rovatti, Emanuele Severino, and Carlo Sini.

Gianpiero had something wrong with his eye; he was always touching his glands. All three of us got tested in February, and his was positive.

Tragedy, fear. This was the first wave of AIDS in Italy. We knew little or nothing about it and protected ourselves even less. In those years people thought, "It can't possibly happen to me" (I wonder if those years are really over; it doesn't seem like it). Above all, those were the years when the "gay plague" was generating terror and marginalization and self-marginalization, and in any case people were dying, it was no joke. Research was just starting. Today's pharmaceutical cocktails that allow so many people to live for decades were a long way off.

We didn't tell anyone for years.

And the first thing we did was to buy a VCR. Instinctively. Make our nest at home. Wait for the end. What else was there to do at that point?

In 1989 the symptoms became worrying. I've suppressed almost all memory of the long intermediate phase of the disease. And yet I continued to teach and travel. It's actually hard for me to believe that my book *La società trasparente* came out in 1989, and two more in 1990, *Etica dell'interpretazione* (Ethics of interpretation) and *Filosofia al presente*. I know I took leave from the university more than once, but I don't remember how often and for how long. In 1990 I might even have been on leave for the whole year, but I'm not sure.

But I can connect the First Gulf War, the bombing during the night of January 17, 1990, with our decision to go to the Riviera for a month.

I rented a house at Beaulieu-sur-mer from a Turinese countess, and we left, Gianpiero, Sergio, and I. I remember the long walks we took every day along the beach.

By this time we had told our closest friends. And they came to visit: Franco Debenedetti, his wife Barbara, Mario and Angela as always.

In summer 1991 we went to the mountains, at Davos in Switzerland, to the famous sanatorium from *The Magic Mountain,* which is now a luxury hotel. But Gianpiero was really ill. The medicines were giving him a tough time.

It's hard to hold things together in my mind. Realities near in time, but as if belonging to different lives.

On September 9, Pareyson died.

But as Eliot has it, "April is the cruelest month."

In 1992, Easter fell on April 19. In April, Gianpiero had his first attacks of epilepsy. In April his mother died. On Easter Monday, Gianpiero attempted suicide. I came in and found him in a garbage bag he had wrapped himself in so as not to make a mess. He left a note too, but Sergio found it before I did and kept it from me for a long time, to protect me a bit from the pain. In late spring we went to a house on the hill that our friend Carlo Montanella lent us. I took constant care of him, always ready with needle in hand.

Yet there were still lighter moments, somehow, that relieved the burden of living that life for a few minutes. Every evening, before going to sleep, we sang popular songs in bed, rhymes in Piedmontese dialect.

Did I hope? What was there to hope for? I hoped for nothing, they had made it perfectly clear to me that there was nothing more to do. But I hoped it would last a little longer. That's what I always used to tell Gianpiero: "Every new day is a day gained, gained for life, for the hope that they'll find new pharmaceuticals, new cures."

In summer we decided to go to the mountains again, but this time to Zermatt, to see the Matterhorn from the other side. A telling incident occurred right away. To get there, we had to park the car at a certain point and take the local train. I had to go and take care of something or other, and I told Gianpiero to wait for me there. When I returned he was gone. We didn't have cell phones then. I was terribly worried. I searched for him for a long time; he had wandered off without realizing it. Fear turned to anger, and we quarreled because of the tension. He didn't drive anymore and wasn't perfectly lucid. Horrible days.

About the autumn, I remember that we watched cartoons on television together. There's a tune I can't listen to any more because I get emotional, "Cielito lindo," about the three caballeros.

I was always asking him: "Aren't you happy to be still here, at home?" And he would say yes. That consoled me for having prevented his suicide, because a doctor friend of ours had told me that it would have been better for him if I had given him another dose of Gardenal and helped him to get it over with.

On November 24, he was admitted once again to the Amedeo di Savoia Hospital. That is one date I can't forget. That day Gianpiero had written "A" in his calendar. There was a concert by Amália Rodrigues he wanted to go to. Instead, he went into the hospital.

I made friends with a nurse, very simpatica, Valeria Grano, who looked after him in the clinic at night, and sometimes at home as well.

It's really sad to think how one gets used to anything. You don't know if there's a limit, or where it is. The limit between what's humanly bearable and what's not.

I recall writing articles for *La Stampa* in the hospital and phoning them in.

I feel a sense of estrangement rereading those pieces today, written while I was by Gianpiero's bedside without knowing that the end for him, and an epoch in my life, was near. He was practically in his agony, and on December 14, on the front page of *La Stampa,* I was commenting on "the wave of violence (racist, xenophobic, tribal, or 'simply' hooligan) spilling over the world from East to West" and fearing "the risk of an Islamic holy war that seems ever ready to explode." On December 20, with the Tangentopoli scandal in full swing (Mario Chiesa had been arrested the previous February) I commented on Craxi's prosecutorial notification. In *Tuttolibri* for December 27 I wrote about the new catechism the Catholic Church had given birth to after six years of work; in *La Stampa* for the same date, one of the endless cases of Palestinians expelled from Israel and refused entry by Lebanon; and on December 29 (it makes me shiver) a short piece on Umberto Bossi. December 29, the day before. I didn't know it was going to be the day before forever.

As long as Gianpiero could still walk, we used to take a stroll in the courtyard of the hospital around noon. There were a lot of cats there too, a colony of hospital cats that we used to feed.

When Gianpiero could only get around in a wheelchair, I would push it, in the garden.

Sergio was around. But he had his job as a teacher too.

The period between Christmas and New Year was the final plunge. Gianpiero went into a coma. He died on December 30. At just forty-three years of age. I'm glad that I helped Valeria, the nurse, prop Gianpiero up in bed and change his diaper just half an hour before he died.

Sergio and I were looking at a newspaper, the travel section. Gianpiero's breathing was raspy. At a certain point we didn't hear him any more. Imagine if he had died while I was taking a quick nap at home. It would have been devastating. But no, luckily I was there. I was there, close to him.

On the hospital file they wrote "exitus." Really: "exitus." Mamma mia.

For the funeral I managed to get the church of San Lorenzo, which wasn't easy because they generally use it for weddings. But in the end I got it. We were in the middle of the holidays, so it was a few days before the funeral could be held. We held it on January 4, the day of my fifty-seventh birthday.

I remember there was a huge turnout. There was no guarantee there would be, far from it. But he had a lot of friends, and so did I obviously. Julio came from Rome too, already wearing a cap to hide his hair loss. He had AIDS as well.

There were friends, colleagues, students.

At those moments it's as if you're in preanesthesia, distraught and only half-aware, it's as if everything is wrapped in a sort of protective fog. Out of that fog I saw a few faces looming here and there, "important" friends whom I'll always remember for turning up: Livio Garzanti, Cesare Annibaldi, Ezio Mauro, Paolo Mieli.

49 | WITH THE YOUNGER SON

If I hadn't cultivated my dream of a multiple family. If I had behaved worse, been more jealous, more adamant . . . maybe Gianpiero wouldn't have gone to that sauna in Nice, maybe he wouldn't have caught AIDS. Sometimes I tell myself that. That is the regret I have concerning Gianpiero, my remorse. But I know that's not really how things are. He and I were both going to saunas already before that.

Concerning Sergio, on the other hand, my remorse is that I left him too much alone, especially after I was elected to the European Parliament in 1999. I pictured him back in Turin having a wild time, but later I found out that Gianpiero's illness and death had frightened him so much that he spent his evenings alone in front of the television.

When Gianpiero died I didn't find myself widowed completely, because I had a good "replacement." Sergio helped me a lot. To live. We tried to console each other by turns. Actually, he was now much more tranquil in a way: with the rivalry over perforce between my two "sons," with the end of the rivalry with his "older brother," everything became easier.

I remember the first afternoon we went to the cinema after Gianpiero was no longer around. And not long after that, to Paris, where we eventually bought an apartment.

We fought together against sadness with the most normal of weapons, trying to make life as undramatic as possible.

In 1993 we took a trip together to Nepal, we two and the two Debenedetti, or rather three this time, because Franco and Barbara had their son with them.

If being married to Gianpiero was a little like a normal Catholic marriage, friendship with Sergio resembled marriage between an elderly couple, affection but no more sex.

Our life together was harmonious. I was happy about him. That he was there.

One day Ezio Mauro, who had moved over to *La Repubblica,* came to visit, and did a whole page on this gay couple that lived together. With him was the journalist Maurizio Crosetti. I recall neither the day nor the year, but my friend Ezio was certainly always attentive to my family life. He had come to visit Gianpiero and me in the house up on the hill, when we were both young; now he was telling the story of a mature gay couple, even if Sergio was twenty years younger than me.

I have to number Sergio among my masters, along with Gianpiero.

Sergio had gone to a high school for the arts and was an art historian. He knew about the techniques of miniature painting, but he wasn't adept with ideologies. For that reason he wrote little. He wrote little and read a lot. He was meticulous. Sometimes I supplied him with the ideological element his work was missing. He could be an art critic, but not a man of letters or a philosopher, because of how he'd been schooled. He taught me to appreciate art history.

Sergio was someone who got me to visit museums.

Since he died, I never visit a museum unless I have to. It's as though that part of my life were over.

50 | THE FRANKFURT SCHOOL

Every time I go to Frankfurt my heart skips a beat. But then, it's only been three years, or a bit more.

When Sergio found out he had a tumor six centimeters in diameter on his left lung, I was leaving to give yet another lecture in Spain. It was February 2003.

I said to him, "Calm down, we'll see what can be done, it's not over." We began a round of visits to all the medical luminaries in Turin. And they all said, "It can't be removed." It was inoperable, so we had to try chemotherapy. But Sergio had seen his only sister die of breast cancer and he wouldn't budge: surgery he would undergo, but not the dreadful horror of chemotherapy. Never. "I'd sooner die."

Sergio was very strong inside. He taught me a lot about our rapport with illness. God almighty, he was admirable.

His mother has told me this story a thousand times. Sergio rang her and told her to come to Turin, where he told her, "I've had a happy life, filled with beautiful things, and now this has happened." He was the one consoling her.

Still, he was a man of forty-seven who was facing death.

His sadness made him behave badly, even with me.

I wanted to be as close to him as possible, he wanted to be alone. Actually, he was afraid of starting to look like a skeleton, he who was so young-looking that he often had to show his identity card even when he was close to fifty. In his last photograph, in his coffin, he still looks young. I was the one who took it, because his mother asked me to.

He went to live in the apartment we had bought in Paris. I begged him: "Let me come visit." Sergio: "If you come, I'm leaving." In the end we met in Amsterdam, because once it was clear there was nothing to be done, he had decided to resort to euthanasia. So we stayed in a big hotel—when someone's about to kick the bucket you treat yourself to the best hotels—and we became friends with an Italian doctor who worked in Amsterdam, Professor Giuseppe Giaccone. But even there, we often had spats.

Before Easter, Sergio grew more serene, and we decided to make a trip to the United States. He wanted to see at least two things he had never seen before: the new Asian Art Museum rebuilt by Gae Aulenti in San Francisco, and the house built over the waterfall by Frank Lloyd Wright in Pennsylvania.

We left for San Francisco on April 9. Upon arrival we rented a car. Sergio could hardly walk anymore. Then the insomnia began. The stabbing pain in his spine kept him from sleeping, he spent the nights in the hotel sitting astride the toilet. It was very hard to obtain painkillers because the Americans have this beastly fixation about drug use. Trips, phone calls, doctors. Once, while we were trying to alleviate his pain, a couple of maniacs arrived. Instead of giving him something for the pain, they tried to take him away on a stretcher. Sergio refused, and so did I.

Wednesday of Holy Week arrived, and we went to see the famous house over the waterfall. On the morning of Easter Saturday we were in New York. Sergio's aunt had given him a hundred million lire to spend. Sergio bought two Carlo Scarpa vases for that amount from an antique dealer. They're still sitting in a cupboard around here somewhere.

That evening we left for Amsterdam to get it over with once and for all. I knew that the oxygen would be a big problem. But they wouldn't even hear of us bringing a canister on the jumbo jet; in fact, they got suspicious and threatened not to let us on board. Sergio pretended he was feeling better, and we got on a Lufthansa flight. They brought us supper: caviar and champagne, the condemned man's last meal. Sergio could hardly even talk anymore.

Shortly after we ate, he got up and went to the washroom. But he didn't come back. The minutes ticked away, and there was no sign of him. I became alarmed and went to look for him. I knocked and knocked but he didn't answer. I called the steward. We opened the door, and Sergio was lying there on the floor. I tried mouth-to-mouth respiration; they called for a doctor who was on board. It was the night of April 19–20. Easter night. There was nothing more to do.

We were only a couple of hours out of New York, still flying over the American coast. The flight was seven hours long. I held Sergio's hand for five hours on the seat beside me, feeling it gradually grow cold, freezing. At one point the steward handed me a note of condolence and consolation. I took care to put plenty of his favorite perfume on him; you never know. That vial you see in the bathroom is the same one I brought home from the airplane.

We disembarked at Frankfurt and the Pietät, the funeral service, arrived. I was joined by Peppino Iannantuono, a friend who had been my assistant in Brussels, and his wife Melita. We celebrated a mass. I had to leave him there and return to Italy. Then finally it was back to Frankfurt so the cremation could go ahead.

Sergio returned to Turin for the last time with me. In an urn.

51 | THE RICH FIANCÉE

As you well know, I've always desired a family. Always.

Right after the Heidelberg years I courted, and spent a lot of time with, a girl, a student of mine, whom I still see and who never married. She's a psychoanalyst.

She was pretty, but above all rich. That she was rich was important for me. My thinking was: only petit-bourgeois people have a myth of "authenticity," because they can only afford one house. Rich people can take broader views. I thought that a haute-bourgeoise girl wouldn't be so set on the notion that you had to be with her and her alone, and wouldn't regard good dining room furniture as the highest aspiration of marriage.

It's not that I wasn't fully aware of my homosexuality, on the contrary. I thought, and still think, that the problem of gayness is essentially a socioeconomic problem.

I ardently wanted to have a normal family. And I miss not having had one, not having one even now. I would be happier today if I had one. I wanted a wife, children, a mother-in-law. And with any luck a house in Morocco where I could have boys. I have rich friends—whose names you would know if I mentioned them, but a few don't hide it so it wouldn't even be a scoop—who live in exactly that way and have done so all their lives.

I take the view that sexual specialization is impoverishing.

I would have liked to organize a serious bisexual life.

At Turin, my "homosexual frequentations" were known. I didn't walk around wearing a sign, but I didn't hide them either. My fiancée knew too, but she pretended not to, or she thought who knows what. And I said to myself: if I betray you with the girl next door you've got a reason for resentment, but if I go with a boy, what's that to you?

The fact remains that we were seriously engaged.

The fact remains that her father didn't exactly see it that way.

He had us followed. For a long time. He went in person to see the *questore,* the head of the police in Turin. Being rich, he could do that. The *questore* confirmed the "rumors" to him, and the handful of episodes in which I had been spotted and identified.

I went to have a man-to-man talk with her father. He said he was sorry, but his mind was made up. He gave a little speech along the lines of: "You know, I can't accept, I am unable. . . ." He didn't discuss the possible unhappiness of his daughter. His fear was that he would have gay grandchildren. He was convinced that homosexuality is transmitted from father to son.

He sent his daughter to London to keep her away from me. I went to visit her with no precautions, leaving normal and visible traces everywhere that I could easily have concealed. When he called Alitalia they confirmed that I had taken a flight to the British capital.

When she got back her father staged a scene, and between him and me she chose—him. And dumped me.

It was December 1967.

Complicated, having a heterosexual family and being homosexual. Yes. Sure. Expensive, above all.

But Aristotle did it.

But that was a different world, you'll say.

Exactly. A different world is possible.

At a certain point, the industrialist Cesare Romiti was apparently looking for an "intellectual ally." And he thought I was it.

It was the time of the Alliance for Turin.

One evening a woman who was a friend of mine gave a dinner for me, Romiti, and Marco Rivetti, the boss of Facis, one of the great enlightened industrialists of Turin: highly simpatico, an art connoisseur, very much villa-with-boys-in-Morocco and who knows where else in the world (but unlike other equally rich and famous men, he wasn't married).

I said some things to Romiti that were a bit extravagant, extravagant to him anyway, a species of extreme Keynesianism. Hypothesis: if a little old lady in New York believes that the shares of General Motors are going to go up, she trades them actively, and if a lot of little old ladies do the same, the share price does go up, people have more money, they buy more cars, General Motors sells more, and everybody makes out.

Gianbattista Giuffrè was another example I put to him. Giuffrè had ruined a bunch of investors. Why did his system break down? Because at some point somebody insisted on seeing all the cards on the table. But everything would have been okay if they hadn't.

I had this notion that the lightening of reality might also be realized through a sort of financialization of the economy, but that would bring money into the system. If I had more money I would buy two cars. I don't think Keynes would ever have maintained this. But to hire someone to dig a hole and then fill it up so you can pay him a wage so he can buy things—it's the same idea overall.

So I put these things to Romiti, and I could see he was a bit disappointed. He replied, "If I go to the United States and I have to change lire into dollars, what do I do?" I replied, "We should have a single currency worldwide, so everybody's in the system." I still don't see what wrong with that idea.

With Romiti I remained friends, and we call each other "*tu*" when we meet. I find him an upstanding and simpatico right-wing gentleman. We call each other "*tu*," but we have a reciprocal agreement to use the formal "*lei*" in public. Otherwise our friends—both his and mine—would pull our hair out.

Since I'm a parvenu, I always wait for him to speak first, you never know. If he calls me "*tu*," fine. If not. . . .

53 | ALMOST A MAYOR

In the early 1990s, in 1993, shortly after Gianpiero's death, politics, direct, strong commitment to politics came back to me, but in a much more direct and institutional way than when I was young.

The Alliance for Turin was born, the local and regional elections were approaching, and people were starting to talk about civil society.

They wanted me to run for mayor against Diego Novelli, the incumbent. He was running again as an extreme leftist, since the Democratic Party of the Left had washed its hands of him. God knows why. One more idiocy in my view. I had a lot of sympathy for him. When he was mayor I sent him a postcard. I had gone to San Diego in California, and I wrote him "from San Diego to San Diego." In Turin he was called "San Diego" because he reminded you of a Salesian brother. They held it against him that he had always refused to have a subway built in Turin, because he was afraid it would turn into a source of income for the Mafia; and in my view he wasn't wrong.

Today we're very friendly. At the time he was furious with us, obviously. The Alliance for Turin included Nicola Tranfaglia, Gian Enrico Rusconi, Saverio Vertone, and my childhood friend Franco Debenedetti—a large slice of the nonextremist academic left.

Actually, my first impulse was that Franco should run for mayor himself, but in a city of industrial workers it didn't seem like a great idea to choose Italy's fourth-ranking capitalist. Gianni Rondolino was with Novelli, and he brayed against me. On the other side of the balance, I had become friends with Ferdinando Adornato, God forgive me. We did a demonstration together, and I also remember a long discussion with Paolo Guzzanti, who supported us at the time.

I would have been elected, because our candidate, Valentino Castellani, did win.

I was a contributor to *La Stampa* (a fundamental requisite), I had the aura of a university professor, a gay one to boot, and I was well known. In sum, I had a lot of angles covered. But I had many doubts, and in the end I said no.

But I was still one of the sponsors, and one of those who backed me was Cesare Romiti.

Our problem was to keep out the crooked ex-Christian Democrats and ex-Socialists who were trying to worm their way in. Once, when there was a meeting to decide the list of candidates, they stationed me (don't know why) in front of the notary's door with the task of keeping the interlopers out. It was great fun.

The only thing that displeased me was to have adversaries on the left.

The current mayor, Sergio Chiamparino, was an ally. He had already abandoned Novelli.

Chiamparino, he's another one. He published a booklet in which he refers to "intellectuals who spout a lot of empty talk like my friend Gianni Vattimo." Thanks a lot. A few evenings ago I took part in a debate with him. He kept saying stuff like, "I'm an administrator serving the city, I have to make sure the 67 bus runs on time."

I told him, "Sergio, okay, you're only a mayor, but every once in a while you might spend some time on politics too."

In any case the Democratic Party of the Left was with us in 1993, with the Alliance. And it was a good experience.

At that time I was a much more of a reformist than I am today. Certainly less disappointed and less angry.

I worked for Castellani's campaign. I showed up for a whole lot of political meetings.

There isn't much to tell about my firsthand political experience as a member of the European Parliament from 1999 to 2004: the lunch where Gad Lerner and Luciano Segre proposed that I run, the slightly hypocritical maneuverings of Romano Prodi, the telephone call from Massimo D'Alema, a letter from me to which Piero Fassino didn't even deign to respond with a raspberry, the telephone calls from Antonio Di Pietro every half hour, the improprieties of Marco Rizzo's stooges. . . .

For the subhistorical record: in the Turin district I was elected on the Left Democratic slate, together with Bruno Trentin and Fiorella Ghilardotti: 130,000 preferences for Trentin, more than 60,000 for me, a shade less for Fiorella. I would guess that 5,000 were for me and the rest for the party; I'm not stupid or presumptuous or ingenuous enough to suppose otherwise. At the same time, Massimo Cacciari was elected in Turin on Prodi's Asinello list.

These are just the little details, minute particulars of history.

The wonder of it was this: who helped me overcome my grief, which lasted for years, at the loss of Gianpiero? Sergio first of all. But also the experience of the European Parliament. Because I discovered a true family. I had an office and a couple of assistants at Turin, and a terrific assistant at Brussels. I still miss arriving in

Brussels and finding Peppino waiting for me, then returning to Turin and finding Mario and Stefano.

So I took an obligatory five-year leave from the university and became a member of the European Parliament, meaning a person with no political clout who gets to have an unusual experience and enjoy a fat salary—except that a large percentage of it went to the party. When I realized that the Left Democrats were going to dump me, though, I kept part of it for myself, that is, for an eventual "private" electoral campaign, which I did in fact wage.

That money. It was used to keep an association of students and professors that was, and still is, called Altera going in the office I had in Via Pio V, but now it's tough for them without that support, although Nicola Tranfaglia and I still kick in a few euros once in a while.

At Brussels I always used to say, "Give me a report, even a *rapporto protetto*." Because, since they can't decide anything, members of the European Parliament try to win a name for themselves by attaching their name to a report on some topic or other. The Commission sends you a measure they wish to take, you study it and write the whole thing up, then take it to your group and present it. Even if the Assembly does vote it down, the Commission goes ahead with it anyway, because they're utterly indifferent.

I tried to get more money for the students in the Erasmus exchange program, but naturally it couldn't be done. I took a stand a few times in the civil-rights committee on things such as wiretapping and bioethics. I got all the left-wing members of the European Parliament angry by defending prostitution, on the grounds that—for those who choose it—it's a trade like any other, that in fact some prostitutes were trying to form a union, and that we ought to be defending them instead of leaving them in the clutches of the Mafia.

I put the most commitment (relatively, you understand) into the Echelon Report, the thing about the electronic eavesdropping. In the end I even managed to convince the Italian socialist group to abstain from voting because the report was drafted by a German Social Democrat—a certain Schmidt, what else would he be called?—who practically stated that the intelligence services are the business of the governments, we can't touch them, just give them a free rein.

I would leave for Brussels on Monday and return on Thursday or Friday. Brussels is death politically. Fortunately there were these elder statesmen of the historical Italian left, very representative and also very intelligent. When I dined with Giorgio Napolitano and Giorgio Ruffolo it was a feast, because they had so much to recount: Ruffolo had been at ENI with Enrico Mattei, and Napolitano had his own take on the whole history of Italian communism. Honestly, I admired them.

I learned so much. That's where I really became a communist, in the sense that I realized once and for all that, when the world is integrated to this degree of controllability, either it has to be run by a "socialist" government or else we're at the mercy of the first Texas oilman who comes along. Like we are now. I formed the notion that either the future will be socialist or there won't be one.

I was a real believer in the idea of Europe. To the point that, right in the middle of an election campaign, I helped to organize interventions on May 30, 2004, in all the European countries, in the papers of all the European countries, on the new Europe we hoped to see constructed. Habermas, Eco, Derrida, and I wrote articles. Even Rorty wrote a piece. They all maintained that the only way to forge ahead was to create Europe. If Europe were to become a real political subject, a state, even a federal state, we would be able to say we had emerged from prehistory. Because for the first time a new state would have been born not out of war but out of the will of the citizens. In fact, it wasn't born. I also hoped that Italy—backward as it is, especially when it comes to civil rights—would be forced to pull up its socks. Another illusion.

I did my best, I conducted all my election campaigns properly, speeches, publications. But at that point the Democratic Party of the Left didn't want me anymore.

In 2005 I was invited to run for mayor of San Giovanni in Fiore, in Calabria, the Calabria where I had roots.

In something I'd written, I had referred to Gioacchino da Fiore (Joachim of Fiore). Down there they have an institute of Gioacchino studies, a small journal on Gioacchino, and so on, and as soon as someone refers to Gioacchino they are all thrilled: our numbers have swollen by one!

I went in September 2004 and found a group of really sharp young people. In the parish hall we talked about so many things: culture, theater, the future, philosophy.

It was easy for me to get emotionally attached to that group of kids. A few months later, with the local and regional elections imminent, they told me, "We'd like to form a new party and run you as candidate for mayor." I said, "If you guarantee I won't be elected, I'll be glad to, so as to bring in a few votes." But in fact there was one ballot for the mayor and another for the list. If I had won, as they expected, I really would have had to be the mayor. I was already thinking about going down to San Giovanni in Fiore for a few days a week, mamma mia . . .

In politics I've always believed in the things I have done as I went along, and I did them with commitment and conviction. But I'm also well aware that for me San Giovanni in Fiore represented the family experience one more time, my invincible longing. I didn't have Gianpiero anymore, I didn't have Sergio anymore, I didn't have my European parliamentary assistants. But there were the kids in San Giovanni in Fiore.

I waged an excellent election campaign, the crowds came out to hear me: a fag, from up north, a philosopher. We weren't playing around. We had a fine long platform, one hundred points, all fully explained: tourism and local trades instead of a tradition of small clienteles living on state handouts; an end to "socially useful" (that is, useless) workers supported by the right because the right-wing candidate was a friend of Gianni Alemanno.

The traditional left, in power there forever, was careful not to accept me as its candidate. So I waged an election campaign against both the right and the permanent government of the left, and nothing changed.

I got 12 percent; the slate got 6 percent. We were more than trounced; we couldn't even participate in the second round of voting. At that point I said, "Fine, since we're not in the second round, let's support the right. We have no reason to support a left that's sunk to being pure powerbrokers like this lot. At least the right has never governed."

And so I made myself fresh enemies. A journalist from *L'Unità* wrote that these people are a disgrace, they're not worth two cents. We traded violent insults.

The business was more serious than I had imagined. I realized I had made a big mistake in thinking, "There can't be any Mafia here, the people are so poor there's nothing for them to suck on." Wrong. There was the toxic waste. The kids had located the places where the rubbish was being stored and threatened legal action. The next day it had all disappeared.

That's how I found out why I would have been killed by the Mafia if I had been elected.

Now I've gone back to being a *libero,* or "sweeper" in soccer parlance: in the newspapers, in Italy, around the world. Back to thinking, elaborating, writing. Being a university professor. I wouldn't want that to be forgotten, because it's not something residual to me. It's my job, my primary commitment.

Indeed, I'd like to be remembered as a professor who was generous and accessible, the way Pareyson was with me. I try. I strive to be accessible and welcoming. But I don't believe I'll ever succeed in supervising anyone the way Pareyson supervised me.

When he died, fifteen years ago now, in 1991, and my career as a fifty-five-year-old professor had long been running on its own steam, I missed him profoundly.

He really treated me as the apple of his eye.

In the years right after I graduated, while I was working on my first book on Heidegger, if we weren't together at the institute he would telephone me in the afternoon. If I was supposed to phone him, there would be a mix-up, because he would say, "Call me at a certain hour." A certain hour when? Then I learned that "a certain hour" for him was a precise timeframe, between 4:00 PM and 5:00 PM. He would get me to tell him how my work was going.

Some onlookers were probably saying that our relationship was baronial, with him as the baron and me as the dogsbody.

When he left for Rome to sit on an academic promotion committee or something, it's true that I used to drive him to the airport on Sunday morning in my car, things like that. But the security and the protection he gave me were worth a thousand times more than those little duties.

We spent countless days together. He took me along with him for years, to conferences, to meetings, even when I said things that embarrassed him in front of other important Italian philosophers. He got me a professorial chair twice. He didn't object to my profession of Maoism, he didn't bat an eyelid at my homosexuality, he, a Catholic to the marrow, ultramoderate, with that devastating sense of sin of his. Imagine, one day—before he knew about me—we were talking about Pasolini, and finally he said to me, "Yes, but still . . . somebody who's publicly homosexual." It would never have remotely occurred to him that before long his own disciple would be "somebody publicly homosexual."

He never reproached me for a single thing, even when I might have been straining the alliances that he, like everyone else in the university system, needed. He always accepted philosophical confrontation with me on equal terms. We wrote essays together, and worked together a lot, and for a long time, on the *Rivista di estetica.*

He knew Julio, Gianpiero, and Sergio and respected them profoundly.

I regret to have to say that he was someone who died of sorrow. His daughter Emanuela, who was highly gifted, died of cancer, and he began to get cirrhosis. But he didn't drink. It was the unhappiness.

His wife Rosetta still practices as a psychoanalyst in Milan. She has always been very affectionate and friendly with me.

| # RETURN TO CHRISTIANITY

The ultimate and most scandalous chapter of my history—and it obviously didn't come out of the blue—is that I became a Christian again.

There are many overlapping reasons.

I asked myself why it was that I adopted a "left" reading of Heidegger, that of "increasing lightness," versus a "right" reading, because one does exist. (And here the reference is purely philosophical, to the Hegelian right and left, even though it was the Hegelian right that read Hegel as the restoration of traditional religiosity, whereas Marx and Feuerbach were out to cause trouble.) Purely because he seemed to me closer to the political left? Not in your wildest dreams. Because . . . I am Christian. Because I am someone who thinks of the good in terms of withdrawal rather than of affirmation. God incarnates himself. Indeed he does . . . but he's a carpenter who winds up being crucified—in other words, he's not exactly the triumphant Messiah.

Here's where René Girard comes in. Casually once again: Marco Vallora, an ex-student of mine, asked me to review Girard's book *Things Hidden Since the Foundation of the World*.

I read a few pages and realized immediately that it was right up my alley. (Girard and I have become friends in recent years.)

I read Girard, and it was like an illumination. I owe him a great deal and am greatly devoted to him, although we differ on some points. It was he who re-Christianized me (albeit in my own way), it was with him that I began to think that it might be possible to bind weakening, secularization, and Christianity closely together.

Girard invented the theory of the scapegoat: human society is an agglomeration in which everyone imitates everyone else, but this imitation produces continual crises. Your car is bigger than mine; I want one like that, too, though if I hadn't seen yours the thought would never have occurred to me. This situation is resolved only when a scapegoat is found, belonging to neither group, like the referee in a soccer match. Shouting *"arbitro cornuto"* (the referee is a cuckold) is a typical example of how opposing groups of fans can form alliances and instead of massacring each other, cast all the guilt onto a scapegoat.

The scapegoat par excellence is Jesus Christ.

For Girard the whole social mechanism is built up around this sacrality of the victim. But he thinks (and the difference is not insignificant) that the mass, the symbol of the sacrifice, is indispensable to keep the originary violence from returning. Sacrificing a victim still serves today as an outlet for social violence. If we secularize too much we are done for, because violence reemerges in its raw form. It has to be bridled.

I, on the other hand, think that Jesus Christ comes to renounce, not fulfill, the sacrality and the necessity of the victim. Jesus is the first great desacralizer of the natural religions. He comes and declares to everyone that it's not true that we have to offer sacrifice to God. On the contrary, God calls us friends. And Jesus was crucified because everyone was so scandalized at the fact that he was telling them that until now they'd only been sacrificing in vain, that they couldn't bear him. He was nailed to the cross because he repudiated the victimary mechanism.

This is such a shattering novelty that it could only have come from "outside." I would even hazard that the proof that Jesus is God is precisely the fact that it could only have come from a nonhuman wisdom, this radically new news. This is not a proof of the existence of God, of course, or the divinity of Jesus, but for me it's a beautiful thing. Almost too beautiful to be true.

I am unable reasonably to disavow it.

Therefore in recent years I have increasingly considered myself a Christian philosopher vis-à-vis philosophers who were mainly Jews. Nothing to do with anti-Semitism. It remains the case that as a Christian I think that history has a salvific meaning: there is a history of salvation, in well-marked stages. The promise of the Messiah, the arrival of the Messiah, and after the Messiah the wait for the Parousia, the return. Coherent Jews like Levinas and Derrida think that the Messiah never did arrive, and they don't even know if he ever will. They imagine him as Water Benjamin does, a sort of "weak messianism": he is always somewhere on the horizon, there is an unending tension toward the other who is to come but who never does come, and who apart from anything else doesn't even leave signs.

I always used to ask Derrida in person, and not in jest, "How do you distinguish between Hitler and the other who is yet to come? Hitler was something so absurd that nobody could have anticipated him. But then, if the other who is yet to come is he whom you could never have anticipated, how can you say that Hitler isn't the Messiah? I can say it because I have the example of Jesus Christ, but you?"

Consequences.

All the phenomena of secularization in modernity, to the extent they represent a desacralization of the sacred, are the heritage of Christianity.

Weakening is a vision of modernity as true realization of Christianity in nonsacral terms.

Modernity interprets Christianity in terms of individual rights and freedom of conscience, all the things against which the Church has always fought to the death. Like it is doing today. But notwithstanding that, for me the authenticity of Christianity lies in modern-liberal-socialist-democratic thought, in defiance of all the popes and cardinals.

Postmodern nihilism is the up-to-date form of Christianity.

Therefore weak thought is the only Christian philosophy on the market. The market, though, doesn't give a hoot.

Weak thought is also the only thinkable Christian philosophy. The Church doesn't realize that? Monsignor Carlo Caffarra paints me as the devil? There's nothing I can do about that, so much the worse for them.

I think that Christianity is a religion that self-annuls, in the sense that it annuls all forms of dogmatism. Hence, God willing, a religion and a nonreligion.

That is the only thing to preach. The other remedies on the market all entail joining up with one side or another: either you sign up with the Christians, or with the Enlightenment fundamentalists, or the Islamic fundamentalists.

For my part, I don't want to enlist. I'd like to sign up with the "debilists." But we're just a tiny handful.

58 | SOME REALITY, PLEASE

My new book will be on reality, and it will be an up-to-date manifesto on weak thought. On reality and the future.

I've given some lectures at Leuven on this theme, and also my university course this year.

I talk about the "Heidegger effect" and the "Nietzsche effect," meaning the critique of the notion of reality in my two lifelong references, but I go farther, much farther. I show that the very notion of reality is violent.

This new theoretical elaboration won't be greeted any more warmly. Because there's this pervasive need for realism and certainty right now. There's a return to politics and especially to religion, with regressive characteristics like a need for facile security, a turning back, an embrace of community if that's what it takes to bear the anguish of the dissolution of the real in postmodern society.

The point of departure is another concept at which I arrived some time ago, which is that my relativism is not absolute. All my thought and all my life are against every absolute, against every claim to absoluteness, which all translate into political oppression and oppression of consciences. So how am I going to absolutize anything, even relativism?

So the concept is the one I've already alluded to: that which is real does exist, but within certain paradigms. It's always possible to establish whether a proposition is true or false, but only within paradigms: a historical moment, a certain scientific discipline.

Now I am trying to take a further step. My "analytical" friends were always recommending an American author, John McDowell, to me. I read him and found him still very much tied to Kant, to Aristotelianism, to absolutes in short. But contradictory at the same time, and therefore useful for me. What I like in McDowell is that the passage to scientific truth is mediated by mathematics. I would interpret him as follows: reality is formulas, not single facts. The single fact proves nothing, at most it invalidates, as Karl Popper would say, with his eternal conviction that invalidation brings us closer to the truth. (A piece of real foolishness: from the fact that a hypothesis is mistaken you derive nothing at all.)

There it is, the step ahead: a passage to another level that is true, but not so real any more. When you put a concrete experience into a formula—a brick falls on my foot, then I measure its velocity, and so on—it does become true, but it is no longer the immediately real. And this is something even I can use: the sciences too are forms of lightening of reality because they transform it either into manipulable technologies or into universalizable formulas, but the universality depends on the thing no longer being there, being present. This is what I've got buzzing around in my head.

Once again there's an immediate translation, an existentially and politically important upshot: politically and ethically, what is best is the self-consumption of everything presenting itself as objective and absolute; of the wall you run up against, which ought not to be taken as that which you have to come to terms with, as though it were insuperable. On the contrary, coming to terms with it means precisely taking a hammer to it. To batter it down means to make the claims to absoluteness of ethical and political propositions lighter, but also to transform the world into a scientific, technologically calculated, system, dependent on the human. If the human is Bush on his own, it's a disaster, but if it's all of us together, it will be socialism. Let's hope so.

And at this point—maybe it will be the very last passage, who knows—I will have to measure myself against the last things, with the things that make one's hands tremble: death, judgment, hell, paradise.

This is what I'm working on, I don't know what I'll say yet.

I was already approaching these themes after having written *La società trasparente,* to the point that when a second edition was under consideration, I added a chapter on "the limits of derealization."

The idea is: let's move toward a society in which image and reality are indistinguishable—the image given me by interpretation, that is.

At the same time technology—and about this Adorno, the philosopher I was thinking of working on after I graduated, and whom Pareyson, God bless him, steered me away from, might be right—is headed toward such possibilities of control that it is unlikely that people won't use it for that.

So what to do? I'm convinced that not much can be done about the uniformization of the world, in the current situation at any rate, under a sole empire, the United States. But tomorrow it might be someone else. If there's a way out—with the end of every absurd claim to absolute objectivity—it's for society to become the place where truth signifies accord among interpreters, not the claim to demonstrate how matters stand. But accord among interpreters affronts too many existing structures: the Church, capital, all the fundamentalisms.

I am not all that confident that the future of the world will necessarily lie in the direction of the weakening of the real, as I believe it should. In this I've regained sympathy for Hegel, but as Benedetto Croce thought him, or Gadamer, who were fairly alike in this: a Hegel without the absolute spirit, without the end of history. Because this spirit that reconciles perfectly with itself, as Hegel thought it, ends up being a ball and chain, indeed it transmutes once again into the contrary of emancipation. Like those revolutions that ought to be over once they have taken place, but that lead to Stalin instead.

The idea of history as claim to continuity, rather than as flashes that generate a new beginning but then don't stabilize themselves as such, leads directly to Stalinism. In opposition to that stands the idea that historical progress signifies leaping further ahead into the world of symbols, of formalization, of laws, of explicitation, of discourse. When I transform something into discourse, into symbols, into words, I do indeed relieve reality of its oppressing and oppressive weight, but I don't move toward the completion of history.

Gadamer in the end is a watered-down Hegelian, like me.

This is the only emancipation I know, with nihilism to dissolve the absolutistic elements.

There's always the temptation to fall back into the myth of the real, what Heidegger would call "the fall back into metaphysics."

"Be realistic," they say. Well, "Be realistic" means: adapt yourself to the situation as it is, accept things as they are.

Sure, I want to know what the situation is too. But I don't mistake that for the norm. Realism is pure conservatism: the datum is taken as the objectivity that science must recognize and morality must respect. That's why Rorty is so important for me, because he's a pragmatist, someone according to whom what is true is what suits us, what's good for us.

Indignant remonstration: so it's only what's good for you? Answer: not in the least, it's what's good for us, for a group, for a society, tendentially for all of humanity. But not because the pope preached it, not because we've discovered it, but because we've come to agreement.

"The truth will make you free" signifies that that which makes us free is true.

Be realistic, demand the impossible. As they used to shout in the streets a million years ago, in 1968.

One of these days I will give a course in the university on the meaning of evil. I've been pondering it for a long time.

Because in *Credere di credere* I maintain that the only meaningful use of the word *peccato* (sin) is when we say: "*oh, che peccato*" ("Oh, that's too bad" or "Oh, what a pity"). In other words: "*ogni lasciata è persa*" ("Everything left is lost," implying, "Never miss a chance to grab something for yourself when you can"). But every missed chance to do good is also a loss: I didn't pay attention to that person who was asking me for something, I didn't help him.

But nothing objectively evil. Not even killing someone with a hammer. There can't be a natural law that says, "He deserved to survive," otherwise we would be forced to conclude that God is a tremendous assassin.

I've come round to the view that the only real sin is the failure to heed the other, the lack of charity. The only true sin is when I don't pay attention.

If I've committed grave sins, apart from those of the flesh (too few) they have been sins of inattention, of hurriedness, of carelessness.

I reproach myself for that, and I repent. I don't know what purpose that serves. I hope not to commit them any more.

I'm seventy, and I ought to listen to you, my dear Stefano, when you say, "Give it a rest, pull the blinds down, quit worrying." I'll pretend I don't know that you more than anyone depend on me, make requests, even demands.

About Gianpiero, about Sergio—and about my mother, my sister, my aunt Angiolina—I no longer worry. But there are still so many people around me I care about. Maybe too many and maybe too much.

I always think I have to provide, provide for everybody. I am the provider. But that would make me God.

I think it is just and important to concern oneself with others. Charity. To redistribute privilege, even on a small scale. But I have a feeling rather of obligation than of pleasure and choice. And the suspicion that all this may conceal a vast presumption. I try to convince myself: you're hardly God the father, but you act as if you were God the father.

Perhaps I ought to stop giving a hundred euros a month to the Moroccan in the street below my apartment to pay for his *marchette*—in the sense of pension contributions, not "hustlers." Sometimes I say to myself: I'll quit. But then I never do.

I will, though. Tomorrow I'll quit. Quit playing God.

62 | COMPLINE

Many accuse me of having cobbled together a Christianity the way I like it. So what? Am I supposed to live according to a religion I dislike?

It's true, I've lived religion primarily as a tranquilizer, something soothing, in recent decades. Where's the harm?

Ever since Gianpiero fell ill, I recite compline, the part of the breviary that ends the day, every evening before going to sleep. I still do so today.

If Cacciari only knew! How he would rail at me from his lofty perch.

A habit? A superstition? But superstition is the only serious thing one can cultivate in life. The rest is just chatter.

63 | THE TREASURE CHEST OF BEING

If we think of Being as that which illuminates things from the perspective of mankind, mankind located in time, mankind that inherits a language and modifies it, that projects itself, then *Being and Time* could be retitled *Being Is Time*. Being is temporality.

Heidegger goes so far as to write that death is the treasure chest of Being. Death as the treasure chest of Being? Is that possible? Yes. Look, how many times can I alter my thinking over the course of a lifetime? Four, five, that's about all. If I didn't die, I'd always be clinging to the last interpretation I had come up with. It's only by dying that we make room for other events of Being.

I don't know if we die for that reason. It's certain that Being can irrupt only because we die.

Historicity means mortality. Without mortality we would all be around forever, and Being would be unable to occur in new illuminations.

Defeated on every front, I've never felt so free.

Cesare Annibaldi (that's right, the Fiat executive) said to me one day, repeating a brilliant witticism of Ennio Flaiano, "Failure has gone to your head." That must be it.

In the end, without ever having acknowledged it to myself so explicitly and so forcefully, I've sought freedom above all else. For me. For others. Perhaps more than love, even, more than fame and success certainly, more than power for sure, I have sought freedom. Knowing that one can be very much alone without being free, but it's difficult to be truly free without being somewhat alone.

Perhaps this is what isn't forgiven me.

Perhaps this is why my ultimate political adventure played itself out under the sign of Gioacchino da Fiore, in the south from which I come.

Ever more often I think back to those two lines of Hölderlin that I put at the beginning of my first book on Heidegger, more than forty years ago: "Only at moments does man bear divine fullness / dreaming of the gods continues after life."

But with the passage of years I've come to think that only the second line is important.

The idea of history as illuminations and sudden swerves robs you of any claim to continuity and absolutes, but it regales you with moments of boundless intensity.

"Are you happy?" you ask me, dear Stefano, in your increasingly rare moments of tenderness. But you already know that I invariably answer you with a smile: "I'm hardly out of my mind."

I could tell you about moments when I've been happy. But I didn't know that I was.

Life is the dream of these moments of intensity. That have befallen. Constellations that freeze. For an instant.

Flashes. Traces. Fragments.

ENVOI

The next day I won't see him until evening. The tape recorder will stay off. And I'll spend most of my time rereading my notes or thinking, lying on the bed in my air-conditioned hotel room, while it's 104 degrees outside, at the end of July with this tropical humidity.

I will go to pick him up at 8:30 in front of the entrance to his apartment building in Via Po, under the portico, a few steps from Piazza Castello.

The doorbell at street level reads "Vattimo-Mamino." Up on the third floor, the nameplate reads "Vattimo-Cavaglià." Sergio and Gianpiero, his two friends who, despite death, have never gone away; they have only gone out for a long walk.

I'll buzz him and he'll come down. Three floors on foot (but there is another entrance with an elevator), above him the administrative offices of the university, beneath him the embassy of Burkina Faso.

Khaki pants and a white shirt with light blue stripes.

I am not seeing him until evening because we've more or less finished. Then too, this will be one of those days. The Professor has a heap of things to do, the tiny huge nuisances of all mortals, paying bills, getting ready to leave for his little house at Nice, just over the Italian border. And there are the annoying dizzy spells to torment him, and a back pain that just won't go away, perhaps because of this rotten weather. Above all, the funeral of Nicoletta, the wife of his friend Nicola Tranfaglia, is being held this morning. Nicola will then come to lunch. And as always there will be his old friend Mario, who has lunched at his place practically every day since his wife died and doesn't need an invitation. And Stefano.

Starting in September, says the Professor, enough of all these people, it'll be by invitation only. But he knows better than anyone that he won't do it. He is totally incapable of not being generous almost to the point of heedlessness. Then too, he wants a family, and today this is his family: Mario, Stefano, Jasmine, the Filipino lay sister who looks after him and lives in the apartment next door to his. Jasmine will prepare spaghetti al pesto. The Professor likes spaghetti, but he doesn't like anyone else to make them for him, even in a restaurant.

Then there's an appointment with German radio, an hour-long interview about the book he wrote with Richard Rorty on the future of religion. Italian television also phoned, and there was a long, amusing, sarcastic exchange between the Professor and the person at the other end of the line, who gets raked over the coals and keeps on saying, "I'm not the one responsible."

The journalist Paolo Flores D'Arcais phoned too, and the Professor tried to convince him to take a position against Israel. Naturally, he didn't even say no to Paolo; he will write a piece for *Micromega* on the new center-left Democratic Party. It will be entitled "Comunque auguri" (Anyway, good luck) and will end—*in caude venenum*—this way: "It's unlikely that those who go to the polls for the first and second round will ever vote for such a party, which is programmatically and realistically aimed solely at keeping things from getting immeasurably worse. Perhaps the Latin American left (comrade Berlinguer, Chile has things to teach us . . .) or some other horde of 'barbarians' will save us. Anyway, good luck."

Finally, Santiago Zabala, his cleverest disciple, the one who will continue his philosophical thought, telephoned.

Another task was dropping by the university to confer with the two final students for this year, and once again he didn't say no.

Although it is evening, the heat and humidity are still suffocating. We set out on foot. It's not far. There is a restaurant he likes a lot, and a waiter who works there has caught his eye. It's not the first time we've been there together. We turn left, toward the Gran Madre, toward the river, then immediately cross Via Po and enter Via Bogino. A car pulls over. A lady sticks her head out the window and asks directions to a hotel in tentative Italian. In perfect French, the Professor gives precise and apparently complicated, but actually simple, directions, as when he talks about philosophy. I say, "You really know your way around Turin." He answers: "When I used to go out cruising at night, you have no idea how many boys I used to take home, in every part of the city. I could drive a taxi. " But he never says, "In the good old days, when I still. . . ." Maybe he is thinking it, feeling a bit sorry about the present, about old age, about the youths who are looking for younger men, but he never says, "In the good old days." It is not an accident. And it is not insignificant.

We turn left at Via Principe Amedeo, and in no time we are in Piazza Carlo Emanuele II. "Here everyone calls it Piazza Carlina," he explains to me, "and sometimes it's even difficult to make yourself understood, give exact directions. Piazza Carlina alludes explicitly to the homosexuality of Carlo Emanuele." A ghost of a smile. We sit down.

Seated at a table outdoors, we finally feel comfortable. Piazza Carlina resembles a city square in France a bit. I tell him that he reminds me of Ignazio Silone, "Christian without a church and communist without a party," ferociously and infamously attacked in life and in death.

I try to pay for once, but I practically have to get down on my knees and beg. I insist. For once, just once, to celebrate, a toast to our shared labor. He always pays, with everyone, however many guests there are. And he could reel off an endless list of persons to whom he regularly gives a little money at the end of every month. Generosity. An atavistic sense of guilt for a financial comfort he could never have imagined, and which he takes so little for granted that he fears: "If I go on like this I'll wind up on the sidewalk and then they'll have to support me." And that ironic knowing bittersweet smile of his flickers once again: he knows they wouldn't. And he tells me the story of a friend of his, a former Russian princess fallen on hard times who lived by borrowing from her chambermaid.

Around 11:00 PM, we return. Fuddled by the humidity and the wine (actually just a glass or two, our toast) we weave back toward Via Po. We look like two overage—very overage—students, and it wouldn't take much for us to start slapping each other on the back. Oh, right, his back. It's really hurting him. Jasmine asked him to wake her up so she could give him a massage. Naturally he won't. Invincible, atavistic generosity. He left a portable air conditioner on, but it won't have got the best of this high temperature, this humidity.

He complains that tomorrow morning he would like to sleep in and spend a whole day for once without seeing or talking to anyone, but the telephone will start ringing before 8:00 AM, that damned telephone. "Unplug it for a couple of hours or something," I tell him. Then we look one another in the eye and say in unison: "But what if it was about an interview?" We laugh uproariously, because a few days earlier he had told me a story, extremely funny and exquisitely malicious, whether true or not, about Norberto Bobbio. Old, tired, and ill, Bobbio complains that the telephone is disturbing him. He is told, "Unplug it, don't answer." Bobbio: "But what if it was about an interview?" Now this surrender to vanity, to the contradictions of success, not so much on Bobbio's part as on that of the human species in general, makes us laugh like mad. Along with the heat. The tiredness. The wine.

He doesn't like to sleep alone, in fact he hates it, but he has slept alone for many years now. He'll go upstairs, go down the long, straight corridor that leads to the main area of the apartment, three large rooms full of books. Photographs of Sergio and Gianpiero in simple frames on the mantelpieces: Sergio with his baby face, dressed in pastel colors. A very young Gianpiero, Gianpiero as an adult, Gianpiero with the cat. He'll watch television, recite compline, and go to sleep late. Like all those a bit lonely and unreconciled to their own solitude, but without drama. Without tragedy.

So I tell him that I had read in the paper that morning about some American research supposedly showing that sleeping beside a partner makes males wake up stupider the next day. He gazes at me, properly incredulous, and not in the least comforted.

At the last turn before the entrance to his building are two Moroccan boys. I've already seen them more than once. They are waiting for him. With a familiar and faintly derisive air: they know he's such an easy mark that if it weren't for the money, it wouldn't be any fun hitting on him. "Professor Gianni, Professor Gianni . . ." They extend their hands. He parries them, trying to act stern: no, there's nothing for you tonight, go away. It's comical. As he insults them, using dreadful language, you can see how fond he is of them. One says, "Today is my birthday." Yeah, sure. With Professor Gianni, birthdays happen 365 days a year. And "Professor Gianni" already has his wallet out: twenty euros for the "birthday boy" and ten for his friend, everybody gets the same treatment, except for the "birthday" prize. He has already given a lot of money to the accordion player who tried to disturb our supper, and he overtipped the waiter—who wasn't even the "right" one, his favorite having disappeared.

The Gran Madre is fully illuminated now, down there by the bank of the Po, where the Valentino Park begins.

Good night, Professor Gianni. May sleep bring you sweet dreams; God knows you've earned them again today. Anyway, I know you'll put up with your back pain for the sake of not waking Jasmine, that Stefano won't even call you to say goodnight, that tomorrow you'll answer the telephone early. And that in the afternoon you won't go to the cinema alone, as you claimed you would, pretending to feel free and relieved. You're one of those who hate going to the movies alone. You wouldn't go into a cinema by yourself these days even if they paid you. You'll prepare your notes and a bag of books. And off you'll go to the seaside.

ABBREVIATIONS

BR	Brigate Rosse (Red Brigades)
CISL	Confederazione Italiana di Sindacati Lavoratori (Italian Confederation of Worker's Unions)
DC	Democrazia Cristiana (Christian Democratic Party)
ENI	Ente Nazionale Idrocarburi (Italian state energy company)
FGCI	Federazione Giovanile Comunista Italiana (Italian Communist Youth Federation)
FUCI	Federazione Universitaria Cattolica Italiana (Italian Catholic University Association)
FUORI	Fronte Unitario Omosessuale Rivoluzionari Italiani (United Homosexual Front of Italian Revolutionaries; the acronym spells the word for "out")
INA	Istituto Nazionale delle Assicurazioni (National Insurance Institute; a branch of this organization, INA Casa, was the national housing authority in postwar Italy)
P2	Propaganda Due, a secret Masonic influence-trafficking organization exposed in the 1980s, with ties to the Italian government
PCI	Partito Comunista Italiano (Italian Communist Party)

PDS	Partito Democratico della Sinistra (Democratic Party of the Left)
PSIUP	Partito Socialista Italiano di Unità Proletaria (Italian Socialist Party of Proletarian Unity)
RAI	Radio Audizioni Italiane (the state television and radio broadcaster)

ABBREVIATIONS

INDEX

177

179